Social System and Time and Space

An Introduction to the Theory of Recurrent Behavior

Social System and Time and Space

An Introduction to the Theory
of Recurrent Behavior

Jiri Kolaja

Duquesne University Press, Pittsburgh, Pa.

EDITIONS E. NAUWELAERTS, LOUVAIN

Library of Congress Catalog Card Number 68–58435

All rights reserved

© 1969 by Duquesne University

Contents

Introduction

This treatise casts its net over large territories. To my knowledge the topic discussed here has not yet been systematically explored, and it is hoped that the present work may serve as an introduction to the study of recurrent behavior such as probably occupies most of our waking time. As J. B. Priestley has recently pointed out in his *Man and Time*, interest in the problem of time has been gaining momentum in recent decades. But probably one could descend even further in time to a period around World War I when established notions about Newtonian time were challenged in several fields of human endeavor. Here reference is made not only to relativity theory, but also to experiments with time and space in painting and literature, film editing, etc. Especially concern with the future, in particular, has increased. We not only entomb time capsules but also planning has invaded both governmental as well as private organizations as argued already in 1937 by R. H. Coarse.*

In this discourse I am primarily indebted to Durkheim whose discussion of social categories of time and space remains a classic today. Moreover, Durkheim was emphatically committed to the whole society, written with a capital S. Though I start developing the theory of recurrent behaviors in a Cartesian manner, the last chapter predominantly is concerned with total society and its rhythm of recurrent collectively organized phases. Because of Durkheim's consuming interest in unity of society, he was primarily thinking in concepts of the part and the whole concepts, i.e., predominantly in spatial categories. My major concern here is, of course, time and temporal dimensions, "the fundamental axioms of any scientific systematization of human experience," as said by E. Bonaventura in his *Il Problema Psichologico dello Spazio*. Though provision has been made to accommodate change

*R. H. Coarse, "The Nature of the Firm," *Economica*, new series 1937 (6) 386–405.

by the concept of innovatory behavior, the discussion is focused on recurrences and their different cycles and patterns.

The study opens with a rather cursory survey of theories of time and space as developed in different fields. Sociological theories of these two existential concepts are the topic of Chapter II. Since recurrent behavior is the subject matter out of which social structures or systems are made, if we may use such a concrete language, Chapter III surveys some sociological and anthropological theories of these concepts.

The proper discussion of the recurrent behavior system, or as suggested in conclusion "federation," begins in the middle of Chapter III. Once recurrent behavior is defined, the discussion leads step by step from individual person chains of recurrent behavior (abbreviated as RB) to interlocking RB of two persons, and finally, in Chapter V, to the chains and phases of recurrences of the whole society or its substantial parts. The core of the RB behavior is discussed in the middle of Chapter V where the size of the collectively organized RB is defined as negatively related to frequencies of recurrence.

To conclude, I would like to express my appreciation to the following professors for their scholarly criticism and editorial help: Albert K. Cohen, Robert Dubin, Arnold W. Foster, John Kuiper, and G. M. Paul.

Social System and Time and Space

An Introduction to the Theory of Recurrent Behavior

I SPACE AND TIME

Genesis of Space and Time:

One of the traditional problems has been the question of the genesis of time and space. However, one implies, by asking this question, the existence of time. Strehler pointed out that definitions of time by necessity are circular.[1]

Thinkers have assigned the genetic priority either to space or time. For example, for Herbert Spencer time came before space, while J. M. Guyau placed space before time. Kant, of course, would treat both simultaneously by locating them as modes of human perception within mind.

Examination of the literature shows, however, that the problem of the genesis of space and time can be discussed meaningfully on two criteria, i.e., the psychological and cultural-historical.[2] Pioneering investigations by Piaget and his students have suggested that structuring of space comes before organization of time. An infant first lives only in the present and the past is known to him only in its results.[3] In the first "ego-centric stage," time overlaps the spatial ordering. The child has to emancipate himself from the domination of the spatial structure in order to develop the concept of time. Piaget's experimental results would thus challenge Kantian assumptions about the a priori modes of time and space of human mind. However, Piaget's thesis about the genetic priority of space was also recently partially challenged by Fraisse.[4] It is beyond any dispute, in fact, as pointed out by G. Jahoda, that dimensions of both time and space are gradually extended in the perception of a growing child.[5]

Although no ontogenetic and phylogenetic parallel is here

intended, it is striking that space and spatial concepts appeared to dominate earlier cultures at the expense of concepts of time. Jammer notices that in most languages spatial terms such as "short," "long" were applied to the description of time.[6] For Pythagoras, numbers had a spatial property; Plato treated physics as geometry. In general, the Greek and other early civilizations were much better equipped to handle invariant spatial relations than temporal variables. One of the dominant values of the Greeks was, in fact, the idea of a finite and stable universe whose spatial and tactile relations were almost equilibrated aesthetically and proportionally. According to Plato's poetic imagery, time is nothing but a moving image of eternity, i.e., it is a link between being and becoming.[7] Euclidian geometry certainly expresses the dominant spatial character of Greek civilization. Moreover, time was structured not only by the Greeks but also by others as a recurrent cyclic phenomenon and in that sense time was bound and finite as was the universe of Aristotle.[8]

It is, of course, well known how, with the break-up of the geocentric cosmology and with the geographical discoveries of the 15th and 16th centuries, the whole closed universe of ancient and medieval worlds and societies experienced a radical change. Theodore Geiger has pointed out that the concept of infinity gained ground about the same time in several fields of human culture, in the concept of perspective in painting, in the chromatic scale of Bach, and in the calculus of Newton and Leibniz.[9] However, the Newtonian homogeneous absolute and empty receptacle space continued its dominance until our century. Čapek speaks in this context of the corpuscular-kinetic view of matter that has dominated Western thought up to this century.[10] However, once challenged, the classical view has been replaced by a notion of the multiplicity of time and space, and their cultural and other conditionings, as pointed out by students such as L. Mumford, P. A. Sorokin and R. K. Merton, Fl. Kluckhohn and others.[11]

What the above brief discussion has tried to point out is that in the development of both individual and culture, notions of space were genetically developed earlier than those of time or at least tended to dominate somewhat the intellectual scene at the expense of concepts of time. Perhaps reasons for this genetic difference should be sought in the nature of space and time.

Difference Between Space and Time:

Depending upon the definition of the two concepts, one can draw different lines between them. One could start with the Aristotelian definition of space as an accident of substance, and end with Poincaré's notion that space can be defined only in terms of relations between objects but not as Newton's absolute receptacle. From the viewpoint of the history of scientific concepts, one can observe that we have in fact travelled from the Greek subordination of space to objects through its emancipation in the Renaissance and its consequent absolute independence on to its modern relativization as a function of measurement. Likewise one can observe that time could be defined as a receptacle in which events happen (though as Ingarden pointed out nobody has yet really managed to explain what it means "to be in time")[12] or through the Kantian perceptual mode, or in accordance with more recent "organic" theories of time represented by the Bergsonian *durée*. Though Bergson would oppose any spatialization of time that one can impute to the concept of dimension it appears as stressed for example by J. B. Priestley[13] or W. M. Urban, that in any definition the dimensional notion is involved, termed for example by Whitehead "extensiveness."[14] Regardless of whether time or space exist as properties of the observing subject, or whether they are accidents of objects, or functions of their measurement, or whether there is empty space and time, a possibility denied by Hume,[15] the concept of extensiveness is involved, whether temporal, spatial or any other dimension. Characteristically, Woodrow concludes his survey of studies of time perception by accepting that time can be conceived of either as the immediate property of our perception or as "just a concept somewhat like the value of pieces of money."[16] Possibly, if one were looking for a difference between time and space, the answer should be found in different structures of their extensivenesses.

In the continuing discussion, our discourse will be kept within the boundaries of the organic and historical time and space of human societies. As is well-known, the 20th Century's advances in astronomy and nuclear physics have provided us with new definitions of time and space which apply beyond both extreme poles of human extensiveness as noted correctly by Émile Borel.[17] Within the particular human universe, space has three dimensions but no direction as such, while time has one dimension as well as a direction.[18] Moreover, spatial data are supplied not only primarily by sight but also by touch and hearing. The latter sense is also significant for our perception of time. Čapek, for example, has built his philosophy of time-space around the sense of hearing as opposed to vision that dominates in spatial dimensions. Although time data are proper to all senses, but remembered with different degrees of accuracy, they appear not to be so closly interlocked with some senses as spatial data are. There is no one particular sense for time data as assumed by E. Mach.[19] On the other hand, touch as such appears to be very closely identified with space; it is an elementary space datum that presents itself almost "raw," without being distorted by perspective or any other factor of selectiveness such as sight. Time data appear thus more removed from a sense basis, since they are more abstracted and rely more on memory. Compared to space data, time data are intellectually more demanding and therefore, there is no wonder that they genetically tend to be differentiated later than space data.

There is one more structural difference between space and time data. Though the eye never stands still and keeps scanning an object in almost a random fashion, one experiences the visual object as being more static and passively enduring than a time object reproduced in our memory. Spatial objects and relations in most instances lend themselves to re-examination. "Reality" has been more associated with spatial data than time data. Time data, as Kroeber has noted, at early stages of civilization dream

recollections and wakeful present were not clearly differentiated.[20] If one considers Bacon with his rejection of historical
and other idola, or Descartes with his emphasis upon the existential present and enumeration of all instances of a particular class,
one can easily relate them to our own day's logical-positivistic
"Protokoll-Sätze" with their "here and now" coordinates. Time
conceived as a function of entropy is cognized again in its present
degree of entropy and not in a hazy recollection of memory.[21]
Fron a scientific viewpoint, past in that sense must be always
presented in a form of present, otherwise data do not meet the
standards of scientific evidence.

Before we proceed with the analysis of the present, or as it
is called occasionally "the specious moment," the history of painting suggests a word of caution as far as easiness and accessibility
of spatial data are concerned. Societies already had alphabets to
record time data, and yet no techniques to record spatial perspectives. For this reason it appears that the appearance of
pictorial perspective during the Renaissance did not follow the
otherwise ontogenetic and phylogenetic priority of space over
time.[22] But to stress the thesis of spatial priority one could come
to our present period and argue that as far as recording of data
is concerned, techniques to record spatial relations certainly pre-
ceded by many centuries the present-day techniques to record
movements, i.e., time such as the motion picture, tape-recording,
etc.

Present, Past and Future:

Grünbaum has pointed out that for physics there is neither
present, past, nor future.[23] Doubtless, physical theories appear
to be of no great help to the social sciences. This does not mean,
however, that one should disregard physical time as defined by
the clock. Without the latter, all discussions and analyses of
psychological or cultural times would fail. Physical time serves
as a standard for measurement of all other times.

There is one immutable fact at the very outset, i.e., the fact
that all times whether classified as present, past, or future, extend

during the present time. Oscar Oppenheimer cogently stated the dilemma: ". . . in order to be true, past and future have to be present. But what constitutes the identity of past and future is just the fact that they are not present." [24] J. Cohen in this connection uses "sinceness" and "futureness" as primitive concepts of experience.[25] Probably one of the major differences between physical and social sciences rests here. Any theory of human behavior which disregards the fact that stretches of physical time are timed intermittently as present, past, or future would in fact reduce considerably, if not fatally, its predictive power. Merleau-Ponty ascribes to time even a basic cognitive value: "It is through time that being is conceived because it is through the relations of time-subject and time-object that we are able to understand those obtaining between subject and world." [26]

To be sure, there is no constant classification of patches of the experiential flow as past, future, or present. There are likewise situations when confrontation between these three categories of time is strongly met, especially between the past and present, or future and present; the absence of strong conflicts between the past and future indicates the strategic position of the present.

The present as an immediate piece of the existential flow poses of course the problem of its boundaries. According to Bergson man perceives in the present nothing but the immediate past. But psychological experiments have brought to light the fact that the present is an irreducible quality of experience though its length varies with particular contingencies. One can differentiate "a point of time" which for vision amounts to 1/10 per second, and for hearing and touch 1/1000 per second.[27] In most instances the length of the present is longer, amounting to a few seconds, and under conditions of a metaphysical-religious frame of reference to minutes.[28] One can note that the present implies that a certain number of "points of time" are experienced as one unit and in that sense, as simultaneous. Notoriously, the operational problem of measuring simultaneity in astronomical dimensions has brought about the theory of relativity. Within the human frame of reference, there are also different institutionalized simultaneities as will be reported below. Their differences are due to different units, if not exactly of measurement, then of perception.

There are thus not only different lengths of present (however diffuse) in most human behavioral situations but there are also different layers of present; a one-layer-present is the immediate attention to the now-here stretch. This attention, incidentally, indicates also a fluctuation not unlike the spontaneous movement of eye that is unable to fix one point [29] for long. It requires a considerable and long exercise to be able to fix the mind on one idea, i.e., on a timeless present as reported by Yogas. A spontaneous perception of the one-layer-present is likely to be interspersed by frequent intakes of references to past or future. Only if the present is highly structured as in the case of the perception of a musical melody that is "a successive differentiated whole which remains a whole in spite of its successive character," is the one-layer-present approximated.[30]

References to past or future in the preceding discussion are instances of two-layer-presents. They are presents in the sense that even though layers of future or past are imposed, the present does not completely disappear. For that reason, it is proposed to call these instances past-present and future-present.[31] Human action characterized by the image of a goal is an excellent example of future-present stretches that are negotiated with the one-layer-present. Or in case of a past-present, actions which have been recently carried out and are relevant to the present or immediately future action, are frequently brought into the foreground. Though a game can be conceived of as a present, it is clear that a player more or less keeps reviewing his strategies in the light of the past-present movements of the opponent. All actions appear then to transcend the one-layer-present by their frequent falling back upon the two-layers-presents. It appears that the one-layer-present is comparatively less frequent in human behavior than the two-layers-presents. The uniqueness of the direct attendance of the present probably accounts for aesthetic elements that often accompany the one-layer-present. Considered from this viewpoint, human behavior then is carried more by past-presents and future-presents than by a pure one-layer-present. Man transcends the immediate present most of his waking time, as suggested, for example, by M. Nicholl or F. P. Kilpatrick and H. Cantril.[32] On that count, if Ingarden speaks mostly about the present phase that sinks into the past, this is in fact a rather special case of self-reflection focussed on the passing of the present.[33] It should be noted that the realization that this stretch of experience is present and in a few instants will be past, is a special mode of perception. While behaving and acting we usually do not grasp the present and past structures in their special temporality. To realize the special temporal structure, it is necessary to abstract from several properties of experiential stretches. Therefore, one-layer or two-layers-presents as such are actually already abstracted experiences.

The Cartesian reflection should then better be translated here as, "I keep existing and passing into the past." Though this level of self-reflection does not appear until later in individual life, categories of time (process-change) and space (structure-continuity) are concepts which, if one may say so, are ontologically primary. As is well-known, their comprehensiveness provides order in the whole phenomenal world. One can also notice that concepts of process-change and structure-continuity are both correlative concepts depending upon memory.

Time and Memory:

We would begin the following discussion by saying time cannot be perceived without memory. However, memory is not identical with time because it retains only some parts of time sequences. Thus memory, and its correlative concept, forgetting, can be conceived of as operators-on-time.

Considering the history of scientific interest in the phenomenon of memory, one is struck by the temporal coincidence of scientific, philosophical, and literary endeavours. While Ebbinghaus undertook the first psychological experiments on memory, concentrating especially on rote memory, by the end of the last century,

Bergson opened his attack on memory conceived as a still snapshot mechanism which is inadequately prepared to comprehend process; Freud and his followers conceived of memory as recording and sinking everything into subconsciousness while reproducing only certain censored selected parts; Proust, Joyce, and a host of others challenged the previous classical and Lessingian view about the necessary coexistence of time and space in dramatic and narrative arts.[34] As in a film montage, one could combine different times and locales within new structures like cubists or futurist who painted and superimposed within one two-dimensional frame, different perspectives and different phases of action. According to G. Lukacs the modern novel has developed "a memory for time." [35] Certainly, the Einsteinian relativistic universe had an analogy in expressive art and literature's experiments with time and space.[36]

Earlier theories of memory represented for example by Hume, conceived of memory as an image distinguished by vivacity from non-memory images and preserving the original order of events. Likewise Bertrand Russell defined memory by familiarity. Woozley properly pointed out that Russell's definition is circular because familiarity is memory. Russell, following Hume, accepted a skeptical position in regard to memory because there were no satisfactory criteria of true or false recollection in memory as such. What we remember is always remembered now, and contrary to Ryle or Ayer and others who accept extra-memory tests of past events, Russell stands at his logically defensible though not common sense position.[37] Furlong stressed "the involuntary spontaneity" as a characteristic feature of memory as contrasted to imagery.[38] Whitrow proposed that the difference between image and memory is logical rather than psychological.[39] The difference consists in recording, which for memory is simultaneous with the remembered event, while the image of the future (a predictor) is not simultaneous.[40] It appears, however, that from a phenomenal viewpoint the major difference is, as George H. Mead did not fail to stress, that memory refers to items that are irretrievably gone, beyond the influence of emergent events.[41]

Rozeboom ends his survey of most recent psychological theories by defining memories as "aroused beliefs about past events," implying that we know intuitively what is past or future or present.[42]

Though memory intuitively defines certain images as past, it is clear that not all memories do contain a strong property of pastness. Most of our learned notions and behaviors lose the date of their learning. They become undated memories, if one may use the Aristotelian term in this context. Ribot in this connection has stressed the advantages of forgetting. One could propose then, that such a remembering which removes the date, in fact transfers the item within the present. Stored in a memory, items are available for usage, expanding the cultural space of a person. Note that many social commemorative events more or less also tend to lose the historical date.

To bring this short discussion of memory to an end, let us summarily review the three categories of memories discussed: first, there is the past-present double-layer memory. Secondly, there is a memory of the past that is not immediately involved in the present. It appears that G. H. Mead overstated his concern with situation and action when maintaining that all memories are functionally related to present conduct. There appear to be memories whose immediate relation to the present is not clear. Thirdly, there are dateless memories that have been transferred to the present, enriching its differentiation. The latter instance is the closest man can come to recapturing the past. It is the past that has been, through the learning process, transferred to the present. Similar processes can be identified on the societal level as will be discussed later.

Multiple Layers and Direction of Time:

The structure of the flow of experiential time has been shown to be multiple. Culture certainly imposes a certain order among different categories of particular times. Essentially these categories are differentiated on the basis of different degrees of abstraction. Psychologically and culturally the flow of time is carried by different chains of units of time as will be shown later in chapters on recurrent behaviors. Nonetheless, all categories of time or levels of units share one organizing principle provided that a person is mentally normal. There is only one direction of all times, because all times are carried by the one-layer-present. In that sense, the one-layer-present is the "reality principal," using the Freudian term. Though it is true that both past and future are also usually following in successive order, as stressed by Whit-row,[43] it is not necessarily always so. For example, within one day, a person certainly evokes memories of different pasts, frequently in a non-successive order. Moreover, social commemorative events refer during a year to events that are not ordered during the year period according to their earlier historical time succession. Thus, both the individual person and society do not observe the earlier historical order of events, and in this sense tend to transfer the memories of past to the present. A total transfer would occur if, as stated in the earlier section, the date of the remembered event is lost while the event remains remembered.

The foregoing discussion appears to indicate that there is a considerable degree of arbitrariness in the successive property of time. Though certainly time does not flow backwards within the human context, particular reproduced stretches of memories do not always follow each other consecutively.

The apparent lack of order, it appears, has been kept within bounds because of for at least two reasons: first, within the particular image remembered the consecutive order is almost always preserved unless the memory has been significantly trans-formed. Second, each of the particular stretches of the past is usually separated by the present. The present then is the organizer of particular pasts. If presents were not interposed between them, the flow of memories most probably would become not images of the past but dateless images or time-mixed images. There is a continuum of images from the dated toward the un-dated. Whether an image is dated as future or past is an intuitive primary fact given to us in a similar way as, for example, our perception of a particular color is an elementary fact of experience.

Since some images appear only partially dated, it is clear that the falling back upon the one-layer-present helps to introduce a time order.

We have so far differentiated different times, all however organized around the present. Differences between these times were established by their distances and relationship toward the present. Essentially the organizing principle has been unidimensional and one-directional, though the succession order has been found problematic. Suppose, however, that instead of looking toward the asynchronic past or future, we look synchronically into space which, so far in this chapter, has been discussed considerably less than time.

Multiple Layers and Space:

Znaniecki observed that social phenomena are primarily time phenomena and only secondarily space phenomena.[44] Znaniecki obviously did not consider population and ecological phenomena as genuine social phenomena. Though in this analysis we will later analyze social phenomena along their physical space distribution, the latter will not be the major focus of our interest.

Space can be conceived of as a function of a simultaneous relationship. The latter involves the concept of present whose extensiveness can vary from "the point of time" to simultaneities of a day, possibly a year or generation. Depending upon the level of abstraction, the time unit of simultaneity varies accordingly. It is of course true that while acting we rarely see our experiences in terms of our whole life, or lives of generations of our society. Nevertheless, the theoretical framework within which recurrent behaviors will be analyzed in the following chapters ought to provide concepts of that order. Recurrences of behaviors can be evidently defined within different levels of abstraction and accordingly different units of time.

The concept of layers provides the necessary structure for different categories of simultaneities. One can imagine the layers as a reversed rectangle which is standing on its culmination point. This is "the point of time," the most concentrated present but rarely in fact realized present. The higher one moves away from this point, the larger extensively units appear. Surprisingly, the so-called theory of the reference group has not considered the possibility of different time layers used in evaluation of particular problems. Bláha has come close to this issue by his theory of the harmonizing function of intelligentsia. Presumably, he argued, intellectuals tend to analyze problems within larger units and more extensive relations, than their opposites.[45]

Relations Between Space and Time:

At this point it behooves us to introduce a proposition around which will be organized most of the elaborations in the following chapters. It appears that what is considered in a culture as simultaneous is not only a variable, but in many instances a function of a number of persons or groups involved. It means that if more persons are involved- and in this sense more space is involved- the unit of simultaneity tends to become more extended, and vice versa. To illustrate, let us refer to a national election that is certainly considered to be simultaneous despite the fact that it runs the whole day and eventually has a three hour delay if both the east and west coast of America are considered. In school or in the Army and other organizations, persons born within the same year are treated as being born within the same unit, i.e., simultaneously on a specified layer.

Thus we are inclined to conclude that the social space which in this instance can be defined by a number of related persons or organizations, is a function of the unit of simultaneity, i.e., time and vice versa. It means that in many instances more social space will also mean longer units of time, i.e., space and time appear as positively related to each other.

The following chapters will of course specify and qualify the functional relationship between both time and space considered from the sociological viewpoint. Compared to the physical treatment of these two existential concepts, there appears one essential difference already listed above. If one remembers the earlier discussion on change and structure, it appears that we meet here a similar bipolarity. There is affinity between past and structure on one hand, and future and change on the other hand. The past, as stated earlier, is irretrievably gone, and in that sense is determined, or structured. The future is potentially here and in that sense is bound to contain properties of change. In other words, this is the old classical and yet permanently new fact of human existence, the being and becoming that has fascinated men since Plato to Whitehead. In developing the system of recurrent behaviors, we will likewise consider the phenomenal world in terms of variable as well as invariant relations.

NOTES

1. Bernard L. Strehler, *Time, Cells and Aging,* (New York: Academic Press, 1962), p. 4.

2. Among books examined the following should be listed in this connection: Gaston Bachelard, *La Dialectique de la Durée,* (Paris: Boivin, 1936); Emile Borel, *Space and Time* (New York: Dover, 1960); John F. Callahan, *Four Views of Time in Ancient Philosophy* (Cambridge: Harvard University Press, 1948); Milič Čapek, *Philosophical Impact of Contemporary Physics* (Princeton, N.J.: Van Nostrand, 1961); J. Cohen, *Humanistic Psychology* (London: Allen and Unwin, 1958); Adolf Grunbaum, *Philosophical Problems of Space and Time* (New York: A .A. Knopf, 1963); Roman Ingarden, *Times and Modes of Being* (Springfield, Ill.: Charles C. Thomas, 1964); Max Jammer, *Concepts of Space: The History of Theories of Space in Physics* (Cambridge: Harvard University Press, 1954); Martin Johnson, *Time, Knowledge and the Nebulae: An Introduction to the Meaning of Time in Physics, Astronomy, and Philosophy and the Relationship of Einstein and of Milne* (New York: Dover, 1947); Alexander Koyré, *From the Closed World to the Infinite Universe* (New York: Harper, 1957); Henry Margenau, *The Nature of Physical Reality: A Philosophy of Modern Physics* (New York: McGraw-Hill, 1950); George H. Mead, *Philosophy of Present* (Chicago: Open Court, 1932); Jean Piaget *et al, The Child's Conception of Geometry* (New York: Harper, 1964); Jean Piaget, *Die Bildung des Zeitbegriffes beim Kinde* (Zürich: Rascher Verlag, 1955); J. B. Priestley, *Man and Time* (London: Aldus, 1964); Hans Reichenbach, *The Philosophy of Space and Time* (New York: Dover, 1958); Alfred N. Whitehead, *Process and Reality* (New York, Harper, 1960); G. J. Whitrow, *The Natural Philosophy of Time* (London: Thomas Nelson, 1961); A. D. Woozley, *Theory of Knowledge: An Introduction* (London: Hutchinson, 1949).

3. Piaget, *Die Bildung des Zeitbegriffes beim Kinde,* p. 366.

4. See Paul Fraisse, *The Psychology of Time* (New York: Harper & Row, 1963) pp. 272–287. Fraisse argues that the young child has intuitions not only of speed and distance but also of duration. However, he admits that "our temporal perspectives, born of the multiplicity of past and future experiences, cannot be the object of a representation unless we place events side by side in relation to each other." p. 282.

5. Gustav Jahoda, "Children's Concepts of Time and History," *Educational Review,* 1963 (15) pp. 87–104. For the reference see p. 100.

6. Jammer, *op. cit.,* p. 3.

7. Callahan, *op. cit.,* p. 190.

8. Koyre, *op. cit.,* pp. 86–7.

9. Theodor Geiger, *Sociologi: Grundrids og Hovedproblemer* (København: Nyt Nordisk Forlag, 1939), p. 429 (in Danish).

10. Čapek, *op. cit.,* p. 5.

11. Lewis Mumford, *Technics and Civilization* (New York: Harcourt, Brace, 1934), p. 17.; Pitirim A. Sorokin and Robert K. Merton, "Social Time: A Methodological and Functional Analysis," *The American Journal of Sociology,* 1937 (42) pp. 615–629; Edmund Husserl, *Ideen zu einer reinen Phänomenologie und Phänomenologischen Philosophie: Erstes Buch* (Haag: M. Nijhoff, 1950), p. 197.; Marion W. Smith, "Different Cultural Concepts of Past, Present, and Future," *Psychiatry,* 1952 (15) pp. 395–400; Francis Ianni, "Time and Place as Variables in Acculturation Research," *American Anthropologist,* 1958 (60), pp. 39–46; Donald F. Roy, "Banana Time: Job Satisfaction and Informal Interaction," *Human Organization,* 1959–60 (18), pp. 158–168; Florence Rockwood Kluckhohn and Fred L. Strodtbeck, *Variations in Value Orientations* (Evanston, Ill.: Row, Peterson, 1961), pp. 13–15.

12. Ingarden, *op. cit.,* p. 100, footnote No. 4.

13. Priestley, *op. cit.,* p. 105; Wilbur M. Urban, *Language and Reality* (New York: Macmillan, 1939), p. 706.

14. Whitehead, *op. cit.,* p. 442.

15. See Erwin Straus, *The Primary World of Senses: A Vindication of Sensory Experience* (Glencoe, Ill.: Free Press, 1963), p. 20.

16. Herbert Woodrow, "Time Perception" in S. S. Stevens, ed., *Handbook of Experimental Psychology* (New York: John Wiley, 1951), pp. 1224–1236. The reference is made to p. 1235.

17. Borel, *op. cit.,* p. 9.

18. See N. Goodman, *The Structure of Appearance* (Cambridge: Harvard University Press, 1951), p. 301. "A concrete individual may change in place or color but not in time." The same point about the unidimensionality of time was stressed by Kurt Riezler, *Man Mutable and Immut-*

able: The Fundamental Structure of Social Life (Chicago: Henry Regnery, 1950), p. 326 and by Max Heirich, "The Use of Time in the Study of Social Change," *American Sociological Review*, 1964 (29), pp. 386–397; the reference is made to p. 393.

19. Whitrow, *op. cit.*, p. 76.

20. A. L. Kroeber, *Anthropology* (New York: Harcourt and Brace, 1948), p. 300.

21. Richard Schlegel, *Time and the Physical World*, (East Lansing: Michigan State University Press, 1961) p. 29. Here Schlegel differentiates between philosophical and entropy analysis of time, plus cyclical and non-cyclical, and reversible and non-reversible processes. Entropy determines here only the direction of time.

22. About the Renaissance and perspective see William M. Ivins, Jr., *Art and Geometry: A Study in Space Intuition* (Cambridge: Harvard University Press, 1946), John White, *The Birth and Rebirth of Pictorial Space* (London: Faber and Faber, 1957).

23. Grunbaum, op. cit., pp. 324–25. See also A. Rapport, *Operational Philosophy* (New York: Harper, 1954), p. 70.

24. Oscar Oppenheimer, "I and Time: A Study in Memory," *Psychological Review*, 54, pp. 222–228, July, 1947; The quote from p. 225.

25. Cohen, *op. cit.*, pp. 95–116.

26. A. M. Merleau-Ponty, *Phenomenology of Perception* (London: Routledge & Kegan Paul, 1962), p. 430.

27. Whitrow, *op. cit.*, p. 80.

28. See for example Yoga reports on "thoughtless states" in which the conceptual notion of time has been disposed of. Kovoor T. Behanan, *Yoga: A Scientific Evaluation* (New York: Macmillan, 1937), pp 214–233.

29. James J. Gibson, *The Perception of the Visual World* (Boston: Houghton Mifflin, 1950), p. 204.

30. Čapek, *op. cit.*, p. 371.

31. It should be noted that several students of theories of time have stressed as the basic difference between the physical time and human lived time precisely the overlapping of past with present, identified by terms such as 'becoming,' 'duration,' 'concrete continuity,' 'overlapping epochs.' See Louise R. Heath, *The Concept of Time*, (Ph.D. Dissertation, University of Chicago, 1936); M. F. Cleugh, *Time and Its Importance in Modern Thought* (London: Methuen, 1937); William W. Hammerschmidt, *Whitehead's Philosophy of Time* (New York: King's Crown Press, 1947). See also diagram on p. 22 in E. Husserl, "Vorlesungen zur Phänomenologie des inneren Zeitbewusstsein, *Jahrbuch für Philosophische und Phänomenologische Forschung*, 1928 (IX).

32. Maurice Nicoll, *Living Time and the Integration of the Life* (London,

Vint Stuart, 1953), p. 239; F. H. Kilpatrick and H. Cantrill, "The Constancies in Social Perception," pp. 354–365, in Franklin P. Kilpatrick, ed. *Explorations in Transactional Psychology* (New York: New York University Press, 1961).

33. Ingarden, *op. cit.*, p. 119.

34. A. A. Mendilow, *Time and the Novel* (London: P. Nevill, 1952), p. 28. Margaret Mein, *Proust's Challenge to Time* (Manchester: Manchester University Press, 1962).

35. Georg Lukacs, *Die Theorie des Romans: ein geschichts—philosophischer Versuch über die Formen der Grossen Epik* (Berlin: P. Cassirer, 1920), p. 128.

36. Indicative of this change are statements found in works such as Arthur O. Lovejoy, *The Great Chain of Being: A Study of the History of an Idea* (Cambridge: Harvard University Press, 1936), p. 242 "temporalization of the chain of being," p. 317, "temporalization of God"; Anna T. Tymieniecka, *Phenomenology and Science in Contemporary European Thought* (New York: Farras, Straus and Cudahy, 1965). Note that also the traditional difference between empirical sciences and "timeless" logic is made void by logician Ushenko who conceives of a proposition as "an operation which demands a succession of occurrences." A. P. Ushenko, "The Logic of Events" *University of California Publications in Philosophy*, Berkeley, Vol. 12, No. 1, 1929, p. V.

37. See W. von Leyden, *Remembering: A Philosophical Problem* (London: G. Duckworth, 1961) for the comparison and evaluation of Russell's "present approach," as it is termed by von Leyden, with Ryle's "past approach" to the problem of the connection between past events and the present memory.

38. E. J. Furlong, *A Study in Memory: A Philosophical Essay* (London: Thomas Nelson, 1951), p. 98.

39. Whitrow, *op. cit.*, p. 85.

40. *Ibid.*, p. 88.

41. Mead, *op. cit.*, p. 3. Note in this connection that in a mental depression a patient seems to be completely overwhelmed by the past, unable to imagine future and change. Erwin Straus, *Psychologie der Menschlichen Welt* (Berlin: Springer Verlag, 1960), pp. 133–37.

42. William W. Rozeboom, "The Concept of 'Memory' ", *The Psychological Record*, 1965 (15) pp. 329–368; The reference is made to p. 335.

43. Whitrow, *op. cit.*, p. 87.

44. Florian Znaniecki, *Cultural Sciences: Their Origin and Development* (Urban, Ill.: University of Illinois Press, 1950), p. 139.

45. Arnošt Bláha, *Sociologie Inteligence* (Prague: Orbis, 1937) (in Czech).

II SOCIOLOGICAL CONCEPTS OF SPACE AND TIME

In a consideration of sociological concepts, it would be useful to review, somewhat extensively, social philosophical and sociological theories of evolution and social progress. However speculatively constructed, most early theories of society were in fact theories based upon the concept of social change. But these 19th century or earlier theories did not consider time or space as a problem. They were taking the Newtonian universal and homogeneous time and space for granted.

Since the beginning of the sixties, a new interest in the problem of time seems to have appeared in the field of sociology. Three works in particular reveal this. First is the dialectical treatise on the multiplicity of different times by Georges Gurvitch, then a general discussion by Wilbert E. Moore, and finally a case of hospitalized persons and their perception of time by Julius A. Roth.[1] In this section, however, we will give attention to those students who were concerned with both time and space, or whose discussion of one of these concepts has been found helpful in the development of our recurrent behaviors system. Clearly, Durkheim should be included in the first group, and his follower Halbwachs, as well as Sorokin. In the other group there should be a consideration of Leopold von Wiese, Kurt Lewin, Talcott Parsons and Fred Bales, and Karl W. Deutsch. These authors of whom two are not usually classified as sociologists do not exhaust sociological discussion of the time and space concepts but their approaches are most pronounced and partially different enough to justify their inclusion here.

Durkheim:

Durkheim faced the problem as an epistemological issue. Meeting the traditional question of *a priorism* of time and space notions or their gradual empirical emergence, Durkheim's answer was, as is well-known, rather ingenious. For him these concepts neither were a priori in the traditional way nor empirical, but they were provided by society, or as we would say today, by culture. Both concepts are based upon their differentiation into units which, in order to become an "abstract and impersonal frame which surrounds not only our individual existence but that of all humanity," must be taken from "social life." [2] One should note that Durkheim made room for "private experience" of flow of time, but argued that the private experience is "far from being enough to constitute the notion of or category of time." [3]

A calendar, taken as a typical time example, and spatial direction classified as right or left, are examples illustrative of social categories imposed upon time and space. "A calendar expresses the rhythm of the collective activities, while at the same time its funtion is to assure their regularity." [4] However, the most audacious proposition was made by Durkheim in his famous proposition on the relationship between social structure and the notion of space. If the camp of a tribe were laid out in a circle, the notion of space also would be circular. "And this spatial circle is divided up exactly like the tribal circle, and is in its image." [5] Though the Durkheim thesis was criticized on at least two major grounds by Rodney Needham and others, it appears that there is considerable evidence that at earlier stages of cultural developments, men tended to impose their "anthropomorphic categories" on the phenomenal world. [6] Znaniecki differentiated in a Comtian manner between an early stage in which men imposed their cultural order upon "nature" as compared to the more recent scientific stage in which man is a part of the natural order. [7] Needham of course is correct in pointing out that Durkheim and Mauss did not submit their thesis to the test of concomitant variation.[8] However, interestingly enough, Needham repeats Dennes' argument which is essentially the same as Cassirer's Neo-Kantian critique of "the empirical emergence" approach.[9] Space has to exist "before social groups can be perceived to exhibit in their disposition any spatial relations which may then be applied to the universe; the categories of quantity have to exist in order that an individual mind shall ever recognize one, the many and the totality of the division of his society."[10]

It appears that a closer reading of the Durkheim's text indicates an inconsistency in his thought, which, also undermines the arguments of his critiques. Durkheim treated time differently from space. He admitted that there is "a private" experience of time, a point stressed by Fraisse. Culture provides its systematisation and ordering. When speaking about the cultural impact, Durkheim referred to the universality and abstract nature of time. Contrariwise, when discussing the experience of space, he did not provide room for individual "precultural" experience of space, conceiving of "right and left" and "above and below" as being equally determined by culture. It appears that while "left and right" are more cultural, the experience of above and below is gravitational and in that sense transcends cultural definitions.

A recent work by Osgood and associates also indicates that there are certain visual-spatial patterns that tend to appear prior to cultural definitions.[11] In any case, the problem boils down to the traditional issue of human nature versus nurture, and for that reason let us not belabor the problem. What is more important for our discussion is that Durkheim made different ontological assumptions concerning time and space. The time order has essentially a pragmatic function; it is a rhythmic organization of social life. "Society is able to revivify the sentiment it has of itself only by assembling. But it cannot be assembled all the time. The exigencies of life do not allow it to remain in congregation indefinitely."[12] Space is conceived of more as a classificatory system, whose "object is not to facilitate action, but to advance understanding, to make intelligible relations which exist between things." [13] In general, logical categories, for example of identity and contradiction, seem to be "inspired by social categories." [14]

This difference, never fully realized by Durkheim himself, is in fact an expression of the difference between the nature of space and time discussed in Chapter I. It appears that Durkheim surreptitiously brought in here the Kantian dichotomy between phenomena and noumena, embodied in his theory of the individual and collective consciousnesses. The difference between Kant and Durkheim is that the noumena were invariant according to Kant, and variant according to Durkheim, although they were variant at a smaller rate than individual consciousnesses. Nonetheless, there is the tendency to deal with process and structure. The former is more action-bound, though repetitive, and less congenial to classification. The latter is more taxonomic and in that sense more cognitive, "reflecting" more invariant relations. Note that the theory of reflection, as developed in the 19th Century by Herbart or the Marxists, presumes that there is a certain invariance in the phenomenal world because a variant and changing flow would not lend itself properly to imprinting itself upon consciousness.

Halbwachs:

Maurice Halbwachs in his posthumously published work *La Mémoire Collective* discussed both time and space.[15] Following Durkheim, he differentiated two categories of past elements, the common that can be easily reproduced out of memory, and the individual elements in whose reproduction memory frequently fails because it is not supported by the collective memory.[16] Even more pronounced is the fact that this lack of social support appears in the chaos of dreams.[17]

An original Halbwachs' critique of James' "stream of consciousness" pointed out that memory could be a stream of ideas but that it must stop, reflect, and eventually return. In other words,

"time does not flow, it endures, it exists." [18] Again this is the
collective memory that helps to transcend the individual flow
of ideas; this is society that "retraces footsteps left by itself." [19]

For our purpose it is interesting to note that Halbwachs tended
to think of society more in terms of spatial relations. Simultaneity
for him was not a purely individual duration. The flow of stages
of our mind has a width that is not determined by previous or
future events but also by our present relations with other
persons.[20] Especially in his *Morphologie Sociale* Halbwachs differentiated a greater number of spaces such as religious, legal,
economic, that are imposed upon the primitive space. Regular
and orderly movements in physical space (called by Halbwachs
the material world) conserve the heritage of society, even
society's *élan*.[21]

The emphasis upon regularity, upon "society that becomes
aware of itself," and the depreciation of individual consciousness
that appears unreliable, if not almost chaotic without a social
frame of reference, discloses Halbwachs as a real Durkheimian.
His identification of different spaces moved him beyond Durkheim. Unfortunately, he did not attempt to show how the different spaces were related to each other

Sorokin:

While Durkheim never raised epistemological questions concerning scientific evidence of social time and social space as
experienced by members of a particular culture, Sorokin makes
a major point of this problem in his discussion of time and space.
Sorokin has been primarily interested in pointing out a difference
between physical science time and space and its sociocultural,
as he calls it, counterparts. Moreover, Durkheim never considered
the locus of social space and time in regard to the physical
space and time to be problematic. From his natural science
viewpoint, it was taken for granted that they were located within
the physical framework; he avoided raising the question concerning the mutual relationship between physical and social time
and space. Sorokin, on the contrary, has chosen to place the

physical and sociocultural concepts into a sharp contradiction. Only in "material vehicles and human agents as physical objects in physical space" do physical space and sociocultural space overlap, otherwise they "touch each other in a portion of each of these spaces." [22]

To understand Sorokin's notion of sociocultural space, it is necessary to list here "the three fundamental planes or aspects" that make up his universe: the first, being the most important, is the plane of meaning. Secondly, there is the plane of vehicles; and finally there is the plane of human agents. Vehicles are carriers such as sound or light. Likewise human agents are social persons that produce and receive meanings. Meanings are not located anywhere in physical or geometric space.[23] They themselves make up a universe of discourse, a universe of pure meanings in which their location is defined in regard to each other. It appears, however, that Sorokin overstated the problem by maintaining that the knowledge of the location of meanings is as definite as the knowledge of the physical object.[24] Certainly problems of interpretation and connotations far exceeded the problems of moving around in the physical space of daily experiences.

The universe of meanings is defined on coordinates of five major systems of meanings, identified as language, science, religion, art, and ethics-law. Together with these five there are five more "derivative and mixed" systems listed as follows: (1) economic position; (2) family (kinship) position; (3) citizenship and political status; (4) personal philosophy; and (5) membership in other organizations and associations.[25] It is evident that there is a certain overlapping between the major and derived subsystems. Sorokin proposed however that these "fields" exhaust any meaning in the universe of meanings.

Faced with the problem of further explaining the relationship of his sociocultural space with physical space, Sorokin uses terms such as "reflection on the screen of geometrical space." [26] He likewise maintains that the sociocultural space is simultaneous, ideational (on the plane of meanings), and sensate (on the plane of vehicles and human agents). The definition thus contains both aspects of his integralist conception of sociocultural reality.[27] Finally, sociocultural space is mainly qualitative and bounds space whose boundaries are determined by meanings. Conversely, physical or geometric space is boundless.

It appears that in pointing out the boundary property, Sorokin introduces a problematic assertion. As long as man remains a creative agent, boundaries of universes of meanings remain open for expansion. Perhaps it is more difficult to accept the suggestion that there are boundaries for human imagination, than to accept the notion of boundaries for physical space. Note also that by maintaining that sociocultural space is nowhere spatial, Sorokin introduces a non-naturalistic definition of society and culture. A general criticism of his ontological assumptions will be attempted later.

The concept of sociocultural time follows along the same lines as that of sociocultural space. By pointing out a number of different types of time such as biological, psychological times, Sorokin defines his time in the light of these main points: first, truly in a Durkheimian manner he maintains that "duration, synchronicity, sequence and change must be defined in terms of other sociocultural phenomena."[28] Secondly and thirdly, he stresses the uneven property of it. It does not flow evenly. Fourthly, it is not infinitely divisible as mathematical time. Fifthly, it is qualitative and not empty time, but rather an efficient time. Finally, it has "a peculiar, three-plane structure—the plane of aeternitas, that of the aevum, and that of the tempus." In a Platonic way, the aeternitas is defined as a plane on which the "everlasting, unchangeable timeless being of pure meanings is located."[29]

Probably, there could be no more explicit manifestation of a non-naturalistic position on the part of Sorokin. Sorokin is here essentially a Platonist, who erects over the plane of processes and change a plane of an immovable structure of ideas. His emphasis upon disutility of quantification is best expressed by his assertion that phenomena such as "courting," "ceremony," "conflict," to mention a few, cannot be profitably handled by measurement because they are durations which are indivisible.[30] Sociological analysis then should be primarily qualitative and structural, and only secondarily quantitative.

Like Durkheim, Sorokin conceives of the phenomenal world in terms of two ontological categories; unlike Durkheim his two categories are not within the naturalistic space-time universe, but they transcend it. The sociocultural space is rooted in the physical space but it also reaches into the non-naturalistic level where it meets the timeless time, the aeternitas, on the same level. While Sorokin is certainly on a firmer empirical ground when he maintains that the universe of meanings—his sociocultural space—cannot easily be located within the physical space, he is definitely in a weaker position when he seeks to remove sociocultural time from its location within the physical time. Sorokin fails to see that a sociocultural phenomenon, whatever its duration, is embedded within the framework of physical time. Both sociocultural and physical times have in common a certain consecutive order, i.e., one direction. Though it is certainly more difficult to determine common properties between physical space and sociocultural space as defined by Sorokin—unless one would like to maintain that sociocultural space is distributed in the heads of members of society—a modern computer with its great but limited storage capacity suggests that one could also conceive of the sociocultural space of an individual or a group as a limited storage. In other words, one could trace here the extensiveness too, though for obvious reasons the extensiveness is more pronounced in the realm of time, whether physical or sociocultural. From this viewpoint, we reach again the conclusion already stated above, i.e., that social phenomena are more profitably conceived of as time phenomena than as space phenomena.

Von Wiese and Lewin:

While Durkheim was firmly grounded within the naturalistic framework and while Sorokin has sought to transcend it, the problem of relationship between these frameworks for von Wiese

and Kurt Lewin is no longer presented in explicit ontological
categories. Though both men to my knowledge have not been
discussed comparatively, they have many common points on
which there can be comparison within the same framework.

First, space is the most important consideration.[31] Von Wiese
explicitly stated that time is only a secondary consideration in
his system. For Lewin topological, life, or phase space, or
"hodological space" were more important concepts than the concept of time which has not been so richly differentiated. Probably the common orientation of these two men toward space
could be explained by the fact that in the twenties and early
thirties in several fields of human culture a diachronic perspective
had been replaced by a synchronic perspective, as witnessed by
functionalism in anthropology, structuralism in linguistics and
aesthetics, Gestalt psychology, etc.

Secondly, both von Wiese and Lewin built their systems in
terms of movements toward and away. Von Wiese was so definite about his basic categorization of social phenomena that he
stated that other movement *"not datur"* in sociology.[32]

Thirdly, if the nature of this space is considered, both differentiated it from physical space but did not necessarily "exempt"
it from physical space. The relationship of adjacency organizes
the system of von Wiese. The adjacency is defined as "simultaneity" of phenomena.[33] Social space is a particular abstraction from
phenomena. It is a "constructed universe in which common social
life takes place." [34] Comparatively, Lewin was more explicit than
von Wiese. The psychological field (space) for Lewin was con-
stituted by a totality of everything which affects behavior at a
given time,[35] with the emphasis upon the present being explicit.
Everything that has influence must be "at present in the psychological field." [36] In the light of the discussion in Chapter I, one
would say that Lewin seeks to bring all elements on the two-
layers-presents. Of course, he meets here also a similar problem
of defining the boundaries of the present, called by him "time-
field-unit." [37] For von Wiese, the present is enriched more by

future perspective and less by past perspective. His space then contains mostly present and future.[38]

Fourthly, both authors used the concept of distance, defined by von Wiese as "arrested approach." [39] Lewin has developed several concepts, such as path, barriers, valence, regions, and differentiation. A well-known illustration of a man standing at the end of a ticket line running all around the block indicates that the man is physically very close to the ticket booth but far from it psychologically.[40]

Lewin in developing his system went further in specifying the dynamics of psychological forces and their equilibrium, concepts never used by von Wiese. The latter in his system proceeded more along the line of increasing abstractness of social phenomena, classifying them taxonomically.

To conclude, let us underline that both these students of space, whether social or psychological, appear to have placed their spaces implicitly within the framework of physical space. Von Wiese elaborated as follows on the relationship between the physical space and his space: in order not to be a psychological space the sociological space is a manifested behavior and in that sense takes place in the physical space. Social space movements between persons are metaphorically compared to a chess board.[41] Comparatively, Lewin was more pronounced on the nature of his psychological space. He manifestly defined its empirical nature by stating that it is "as real" as a physical one.[42]

Parsons and Bales:

We have seen in the above comparison of von Wiese and Lewin that the latter resolved the problem concerning the relationship of physical and psychological space by simply maintaining, without further elaboration, that both coexist in their own right, and that both are empirical. On the other hand, von Wiese was led to the conclusion that sociological space is space only metaphorically defined. Such a definition sheds less light on the nature of his concept of space.

Parsons and Bales have started their presentation of action space by a cautious remark that the idea had been suggested to them by a mathematician. They stated that they would consider their space "to be a four-dimensional space in the mathematical sense of the term." [43] They also assumed that the space defined is "Euclidean" in the sense that it is orthogonal, i.e., a movement on one or more of the four dimensions of the space does not show any change on one or more of the parallel dimensions. Moreover, they made a strong assumption, strong at least for most social science phenomena, that there is a continuous linear variation, and that time enters into the analysis of process in essentially the same way that it does in classical mechanics.[44] Compared to von Wiese's definition of space as a metaphor, this pronouncement is certainly more audacious.

The four dimensions that define space are the well-known four functional problems of action developed by Parsons, i.e., adaptation, goal-gratification, integration, and latency. The dimensions are also defined in terms of the four pattern-variables, too well-known to be repeated here.

Movement in space is defined as "the changing state of the system through some interval in time, when its movement in a given dimension is maximized relative to its movement in the other three dimensions." [45] Since movement on all dimensions cannot be maximized at one point of time, there is a certain time order in preponderance of particular dimensions.

Movement goes through phases for larger systems and through orbits for smaller systems which are contained within the former larger one. In our judgment, this Gulliver theme notion (to use Čapek's terms), is a very fruitful one. The whole action space is conceived of as being filled by encapsulated systems whose units go through the same phases (defined on the same dimensions) but not necessarily at the same rates.[46] Thus, while within a social system of a group an act can be classified primarily on the expressive dimension, within the personality system of the producer of this act, it can appear instrumental.

It is obvious that the action space with its phases or smaller orbits is within the physical space though it is not the latter. The action space is thought to be only indirectly indicated by behaviors (behavioral space). From behaviors one can infer changes in the directly unobservable action space.[47]

What is the significance of Parsons and Bales action space as far as it has been developed by them? First, one should note that a movement in the action space is in fact nothing but a change of property, as stated by the authors themselves.[48] If this is so, why is the concept introduced especially if it is introduced in a very involved language in which the behavioral space sometimes is interchangeably used with action space or almost dropped? [49]

There appear to be reasons in favor as well as against the usefulness of the action space concept. In favor one can list the encapsulation model which helps to conceive of a particular act as being related to different systems at the same time. As it has been stressed above, the outlay of these larger or smaller systems in terms of the action space makes it feasible for us to not only grasp simultaneous relations in reference to different systems, but also simultaneous, though not synchronic, processes. It appears that the authors have not really exhausted all finer possibilities contained in the action space.

Considered from the negative viewpoint, it is clear that Parsons and Bales have not elaborated on the coordination between the action space and behavioral space satisfactorily. They themselves at one point express a desire to have a spatial model of their action space.[50] Comparatively, Lewin's life space is more empirical and Lewin himself never felt a need to translate psychological forces, barriers and distances and other concepts into other space than the psychological one. Probably the interweaving of behavioral space elements with those of the action space is due to the cooperation of Parsons (action space) with Bales (behavioral space).[51]

If one considers possibilities of improving on the unsatisfactory situation, one is struck by the fact that both behavioral and action space have one dimension in common, namely time. This is in fact the fifth dimension. [One could argue that affectivity and affective neutrality comprise the time dimension but this has been only suggested by Parsons and never in fact resolved].[52] Time in fact is the major coordinate between action space and behavioral space. The authors never raise any doubts that processes in both spaces are thought of according to the clock. This helps to increase the intelligibility of both spaces whose involved description taxes considerably the reader's understanding.

Deutsch:

After Sorokin's "spaceless" sociocultural space, Lewin's psychological space, and the Parsons-Bales action space, Deutsch has presented us with a model of decision-making built in a computer's technology terms. Though he has not been concerned with space and time as such, implicitly he uses both concepts in a way that deserves to be considered.

For Deutsch the smallest unit in his system is a message, a bit of information. The latter is defined as a "patterned relationship between events." [53] Information is, however, nothing spaceless, it exists somewhere in the system, either being moved through channels or stored in the memory. Similarly "meaning is a physical position in a sequence of events." [54] Therefore memory is also a physical process described in seven steps: (1) abstraction or coding of incoming information; (2) storage of this information; (3) dissociation of some of this information from the rest; (4) recall of some of these dissociated items; (5) recombination of some of these items; (6) new abstraction from the recombined items to create novelty; and (7) transmission of the new item to storage or to application to action. Note that in addition to transferring and storing, another term frequently used here is "combination" or "recombination," or in other contexts "rearrangement." Thus essentially this cultural or psychological space is conceived of as a spatial-temporal structure of items of information that are organized and stored in a certain order that can be retrieved with certain delays. Deutsch speaks of depth of memory screens that interfere with the intake of items or their reproduction from the memory storage. Government, consequently, also can be conceived of in terms of information intakes, storages, their scope of availability and their recombinations for finding new solutions. What we would usually describe as action, in Deutsch's system are processes dealing with information, i.e., transfers of meanings. Consciousness is then defined as "a simultaneous or nearly simultaneous interaction of a number of different secondary symbols." [55] The latter are symbols that help to classify and order information carrying symbols. By defining consciousness as a simultaneous relationship between a greater number of items, organized on a higher level of abstraction, Deutsch thinks of it in terms of a spatial structure whose parts are in communication with each other, within one span of attention. It is "a condensed and concentrated arrangement of secondary symbols." [56]

It is probably unnecessary to continue further with the presentation of Deutsch's concepts. Though the concept of delay also plays a certain role, essentially, time is not the major focus in his spatial model of memory or government. The major concept is simultaneity—space, the ability to mobilize and confront a mass of information relevant to a particular problem. The Bergsonian *durée* appears irrelevant to Deutsch's notion of communication-information space. However, Deutsch's thought is not mechanistic. There is permanently going on learning, rearranging of patterns; mind is conceived to be "a single run machine," [57] a concept that we will challenge by our concept of recurrent behavior. Deutsch conceives of human mind or of government as a mechanism that is able to steer itself more or less permanently, to redirect itself, to reorganize and learn. Though using mechanistic terminology, the communication theory makes its scheme responsive to "historical uniqueness."

Conclusion:

Such a survey of concepts of space and time, as developed by these eight theorists, reveals differences within their treatment of space as compared to time. Considerably more attention has been paid to space than time. Concepts of space have been developed into a more differentiated structure of concepts. Following Bergson, one could say that the theorists find it easier to think in spatial terms than in temporal terms.

A comparison of these concepts of space show that Durkheim's concern is with the genetic problem of space as a category of human mind, and his follower Halbwachs with identification of different spaces. In contrast to Durkheim's naturalism, Sorokin offers a radical solution by developing a concept of "sociocultural spaceless space." Note that Sorokin dichotomizes the concept of space in a manner not thought of by Durkheim. Consecutively, for von Wiese social space is an analytical sociological concept around which all other sociological concepts are systematically developed. The trend to move away from one naturalistic notion of space is further carried forward by Lewin who, however, is close to phenomenal experience. Parsons and Bales on the other hand move away from the phenomenal experience by differentiating between the behavioral space and the action space. Deutsch uses the computer analogy to conceptualize his implied notion of a communication-information space.

Time is treated by Durkheim as a function of activities, and not only as a classificatory cognitive category. Halbwachs stresses the ordering and essentially transcendent nature of social time as compared to the individual stream of consciousness. Sorokin thinks of his sociocultural time as being organized along an ontology of eternity and change. Sorokin obviously moves into the realm of metaphysics. Von Wiese practically eliminates time from its system while Lewin leaves room for the psychological perception of time; the Lewin's program however eliminates a major concern with time. Parsons and Bales imply time in most of their propositions; Deutsch also implies time and occasionally discusses it in terms of delay. On the whole, with the exception of Sorokin, all authors treat time in terms of the physical clock time or place their particular time within the framework of the clock time. We can conclude once more that time has not really been given as much attention as space.

In bringing this chapter to an end, it is helpful to recall that the problem of recurrence of behaviors has not been explicitly considered at a significant length by any of the theoreticians. No attention has been spent on the discussion of different rates of recurrent behaviors. This problem will be considered in the following chapter.

NOTES

1. Georges Gurvitch, *The Spectrum of Social Time* (Dordrecht, Holland: D. Reidel, 1964); Wilbert E. Moore, *Man, Time and Society* (New York: John Wiley, 1963); Julius A. Roth, *Timetables: Structuring the Passage of Time in Hospital Treatment and Other Careers* (Indianapolis: Bobbs-Merrill, 1963). One should refer here to a more recent study of the extensiveness of space by Gurvitch. See Georges Gurvitch, "Les Variations des Perceptions Collectives des Étendues," *Cahiers Internationaux de Sociologie* (11) 1964, pp. 79–106. The interest in the problem of time and space is manifested by two recent French articles: Jean-Pierre Vernant, "Espace et Organisation Politique en Grèce Ancienne," *Annales: Économies, Sociétés, Civilisations* (20) 1965, pp. 576–595; Rudolf Rezschazy, "Les Facteurs Socio-culturels du Développement: L'exemple de la Notion Sociale du Temps," *Esprit* (33) 1965, pp. 21–44. See also Gosta Carlsson, "Time and Continuity in Mass Attitude Change," *Public Opinion Quarterly* (21) 1961, pp. 1–15.
2. Émile Durkheim, *The Elementary Forms of the Religious Life* (Glencoe, Ill.: The Free Press, n.d.), p. 10.
3. *Ibid.*
4. *Ibid.*
5. *Ibid.*, pp. 11–12.
6. See introduction by Rodney Needham in Émile Durkheim and Marcel Mauss, *Primitive Classification* (Chicago: The University of Chicago Press, 1963).
7. Florian Znaniecki, *Cultural Sciences: Their Origin and Development* (Urbana: University of Illinois Press, 1952), pp. 66–92.
8. Durkheim, Primitive Classification, *op. cit.*, p. XVI.
9. Ernst Cassirer, *Substance and Function and Einstein's Theory of Relativity* (Chicago: The Open Court Publ., 1923), pp. 17–25.
10. Durkheim, Primitive Classification, *op. cit.*, p. XXVII.
11. Charles Osgood, "Studies on the Generality of Affective Meaning

System," *American Psychologist* No. 1 (17), pp. 10–28. Even Whorf, one of the major proponents of cultural relativism, admits that the apprehension of space is probably given substantially in the same manner irrespective of language. What varies is the concept of space. See Benjamin Whorf, "Relation of Thought and Behavior to Language," pp. 75–93 in Leslie Spier *et al.*, eds., *Language, Culture and Personality: Essays in Memory of Edward Sapir* (Menasha, Wisc.: Sapir Memorial Publication Fund, 1941). The reference is made to p. 92 and ff.

12. Durkheim, Elementary Forms, *op. cit.*, p. 349.

13. Durkheim, Primitive Classification, *op. cit.*, p. 81.

14. Edward A. Tiryakian, *Sociologism and Existentialism: Two Perspectives on the Individual and Society* (Englewood Cliffs: Prentice-Hall, 1962), p. 38.

15. Maurice Halbwachs, *La Mémoire Collective* (Paris: Presses Universitaires de France, 1950).

16. *Ibid.*, pp. 30–31.

17. Maurice Halbwachs, *Les Cadres Sociaux de la Mémoire* (Paris: F. Alcan, 1925), p. 276.

18. Halbwachs, *La Mémoire Collective*, p. 127.

19. *Ibid.*, p. 125.

20. *Ibid.*, p. 92.

21. Maurice Halbwachs, *Morphologie Sociale* (Paris: A. Colin, 1946), p. 204.

22. Pitirim A. Sorokin, *Sociocultural Causality, Space, Time* (Durham, N.C.: Duke University Press, 1943), p. 155.

23. *Ibid.*, p. 123.

24. *Ibid.*, p. 124.

25. *Ibid.*, p. 133.

26. *Ibid.*, pp. 137–8, footnote No. 56.

27. *Ibid.*, p. 139.

28. *Ibid.*, p. 171.

29. *Ibid.*, p. 215.

30. *Ibid.*, p. 204.

31. Leopold von Wiese, *Allgemeine Soziologie* (München: von Duncker and Humblot, 1924), Vol. 1, p. 30.

32. *Ibid.*, p. 11.

33. *Ibid.*, p. 30.

34. Vol. II, *Ibid.*, p. 44.

35. Kurt Lewin, *Field Theory in Social Science; Selected Theoretical Papers*. Dorwin Cartwright, ed. (New York: Harper Torchbooks, 1964), p. 241.

36. *Ibid.*, p. XIII.

37. *Ibid.*, p. 52.

38. Von Wiese, Vol. I., *op. cit.*, p. 31.

39. *Ibid.*, p. 179.

40. Chris Argyris, *An Introduction to Field Theory and Interaction Theory* (New Haven: Labor and Management Centre, Yale University, 1952), pp. 8–9.

41. Von Wiese, Vol. II, *op. cit.*, pp. 10–11.

42. Lewin, *op. cit.*, p. 151.

43. Talcott Parsons, Robert F. Bales and Edward A. Shils, *Working Papers in the Theory of Action* (Glencoe, Ill.: The Free Press, 1953), p. 85.

44. *Ibid.*, pp. 85–86.

45. *Ibid.*, p. 181.

46. *Ibid.*, p. 176.

47. *Ibid.*, p. 87.

48. *Ibid.*, p. 166.

49. *Ibid.*, p. 92 and ff.

50. *Ibid.*, p. 200.

51. *Ibid.*, p. 88 and p. 233 and ff.

52. Charles P. Loomis and Zona K. Loomis, *Modern Social Theories: Selected American Writers* (Princeton, New Jersey: D. Van Nostrand, 1961), p. 344.

53. Karl W. Deutsch, *The Nerves of Government: Models of Political Communication and Control* (Glencoe, Ill.: The Free Press, 1963), p. 82.

54. *Ibid.*, p. 141.

55. *Ibid.*, p. 202.

56. *Ibid.*, p. 101.

57. *Ibid.*, p. 137.

III STRUCTURE, SOCIAL SYSTEM AND RECURRENT BEHAVIOR

It has been suggested that social scientists have not given sufficient attention to recurrent behavior. But a good portion of this chapter will be devoted to an attempt to show that widely used concepts of social structure and social system imply recurrent behaviors. Until in the second part of this chapter, there will be introduced a specific aspect of recurrent behaviors that, to my knowledge, has not yet been treated by social theorists.

A perusal of literature shows that students occasionally with explicitness define social structure and social system as phenomena that are relatively permanent and continuous on one occasion. Parsons defines social system as "a mode of organization of action elements relative to the persistence or ordered processes of change of the interaction patterns of a plurality of individual actors." [1] Levy speaks about social structure as being that aspect of empirical phenomena divorced from time.[2] The same timeless aspect of social structure is stressed by Firth according to whom "continuity is essentially one of repetition," [3] Nadel in his helpful discussion of the concept of social structure explicitly uses terms such as "repetitiveness, recurrence, invariance." [4] As a matter of historical interest it should of course be listed here that Gabriel Tarde in his well-known social system that was based upon the notion of imitation, stressed repetition together with opposition and innovation, as the three basic social processes.[5]

In Fairchild's *Dictionary of Sociology*, one finds that structure is defined as: "a relatively permanent or persistent organization of parts" and system as a "harmony in operation and the integration of its structure." [6] In Winnick's *Dictionary of Anthropology* structure is similarly defined as "the ordered relation which the parts of a society have to each other, seen from a reasonably long-range point of view." [7]

Though the above references certainly do not exhaust all definitions of the two concepts, they indicate that social structure and social system are also summary terms for recurrent phenomena, or as stated by M. Fortes "a sum of processes in time." [8]

Since both terms frequently have been used interchangeably, one can raise the question whether one of them should not be dropped. As a matter of historical interest one should record here that the first to introduce the concept of system in the study of social phenomena was probably Lewis B. Morgan in his taxonomic study of systems of kinship relations.[9] The concept of structure was introduced first by Herbert Spencer, although one of the proponents of the notion of social structure in British social anthropology, A. R. Radcliffe-Brown, placed the beginning as far back as Montesquieu.[10] Thus, if one would at a considerable risk propose that sociologists have been more concerned with the social system, while anthropologists, especially British social anthropologists, with social structure, one should take cognizance of the historical beginnings of both terms, initiated by members of the different disciplines

Coming back to the difference between the terms, it appears that "system" always contains "structure" but not all structures can be conceived as systems. In other words, structure is a more general concept than system. This differentiation, in my judgement, is useful and consequently should be preserved. To illustrate it, let us refer to Firth's question as to what degree we can make a system out of certain recurrences of behaviors called structure.[11] Or, one would refer to Nadel's differentiation between model and structure. "Usually, the word 'model' implies more than this, namely 'a picture' so constructed that it has logical necessity and explanatory power, in order that verifiable deductions can be made from it. I do not think that social structure satisfies this latter, more rigorous, condition." [12] Loomis in his taxonomy of sociological concepts indicates that structure is a part of the social system. "Interaction tends to develop certain uniformities over time, some of which tend to persist. As they are orderly and systematic, they can be recognized as social systems. Because the social system is composed of identifiable and interdependent parts it is said to possess social structure." [13] Parsons stresses the boundary as the necessary property of system in comparison to structure: "In so far as boundaries in this sense do not exist, it is not possible to identify a set of interdependent phenomena as a system." [14] Structure, on the other hand, is defined by Parsons as a set of interdependent phenomena showing "sufficiently definite patterning and stability over time." [15] Recalling Parsons' definition of social system, one can conclude that social system can show ordered change and has definite boundaries while structure has relatively less definite boundaries but shows a greater stability. One should note that relative terms are employed, and that under certain conditions a phenomenon conceptualized as a structure can experience change whose results could be labelled as system. In referring to structure, Gurvitch uses the term destructuralization to describe opposite changes.[16] We then could go further and propose that a homogeneous phenomenon that differentiates itself gradually into parts structuralizes itself or, when it returns to its prior state, destructuralizes itself. Once the structured phenomenon is able to interact with the environment in a more or less unified manner, the phenomenon has systematized itself and vice versa desystematized itself. Of course one can note that underlying such an encapsulation model of the phenomenal reality is the concept of different degrees of entropy elaborated in the field of biological and social phenomena especially by von Bertalanffy and his coworkers in the *General Systems* group.[17]

Since the intention here is not to discuss the concepts of social structure and system as such, but only as far as they are relevant to our theory of recurrent behaviors, we will proceed by reviewing particular usages of these concepts in reference to the theoretical framework. Interestingly, the following four dimensions not only appear to have covered all the major controversies related to the two concepts, but they also can be placed within the two existential dimensions of time and space. For that reason the term "dimensions" is used explicitly here instead of categories.

There is first the dimension of the existential locus on which students differ as to whether the concepts refer to phenomena or to analytical operations of the mind only. Second, there is the dimension of parts and their extensiveness also called elements, units, etc. Third, there is the dimension of the modus of the transaction-relationship between the parts that, in terms of time can be genetic-historical-causal, or simultaneous-functional, or telic-future. In terms of space the transaction can be conceived of as covering the totality of the space (a natural science relationship in the manner of Laplace), majority of the space (statistical distribution), or a unique point in the space (historical uniqueness). Intensity of the relationship, which is usually treated as a separate category, in our system is the interval density of the relationship, to be explained below. Fourth, there is the degree of recurrence or its absence, i.e., change.

Existential locus:

Interestingly enough the argument here has been carried on in recent years predominantly by anthropologists. To a sociologist today, traditional questions regarding "where society is" appear to be only historically relevant. Concepts of structure or system, as used by sociologists today, appear to be "neutral" in regard to the existential locus problem. It should be noted, however, as suggested by Merleau-Ponty, that the notion of structure can be considered as a substitute for the notion of essence.[18] If so, then the ontological problem of social phenomena could not be disregarded by sociologists.

Turning to anthropology, we find on one hand Radcliffe-Brown, Evans-Pritchards and Nadel for whom social structure exists "out there," and Leach or Lévi-Strauss for whom the structure is to be found only in the heads of observed persons or of researchers. Specifically, Leach has led a strong attack on Durkheimian influence within British anthropology, challenging Radcliffe-Brown's notion of structural equilibrium. Essentially, when reading his "Introduction" one sees that Leach is struggling with the ontology of social phenomena, and with issues of the phenomenal process and scientific abstraction.[19] Likewise for Lévi-Strauss what exist are social relations only and structure is nothing but a model,[20] or even better, a property of the method rather than of the object.[21] In reply, Nadel points out that while according to these definitions structure is nothing but an explanatory principle, "social structure, of whatever degree of refinement, 'should be' still the social reality itself, or an aspect of it, not the logic behind it." [22]

As far as the ontology of social system is concerned, the issue has been in fact discussed in a prior chapter in connection with the notions of social space and time. Sorokin, who has contributed significantly to the introduction of the system concept into sociology, has certainly faced the ontological problem in his notion that sociocultural space is spaceless, i.e., it means also that the cultural system is primarily to be located in other than spatial dimensions. Parsons, who accepted Sorokin's differentiation between the three systems (cultural system, social system and personality system), defined the latter two concepts as behavioral systems, while the cultural system is "an abstract system." [23] Thus, it appears that while anthropologists do not differentiate at all or not that strongly between social and cultural systems, or for that matter structure, sociologists have tended to split the ontological issue by ascribing the time-space properties to the social system and leaving as problematical the locus of the cultural system. Debates between Kluckhohn and Chappel and a host of others, as to whether culture is behaviors or only "design for living" certainly are relevant in this connection.[24] Keeping this in mind, one could perhaps then qualify the former statement concerning the lack of sociological interest in the "locus" problem.

Parts and their Extensiveness:

Both in reference to structure as well as system we find a great number of definitions regarding what constitutes the smallest unit. As far as structure is concerned, for Radcliffe-Brown the smallest units are simply persons. For Evans-Pritchard, these are groups and explicitly not persons. Eggan sees the smallest units in interpersonal relations, and Leach sees them in ideas persons have about distribution of social power.[25]

The question of the smallest unit has been fervently discussed by sociologists again in an earlier period. For Comte the smallest unit was family, and for Spencer, the individual. Gradually, one has moved away from these more tangible items to the concept of relationship as defined in von Wiese's *Beziehungslehre*, whose German term handsomely says that this is a science of relations. Sorokin who criticized the search for the smallest unit as a mechanistic imitation of natural science,[26] however tends to conceive of particular meanings as the most important items in the sociological inquiry. But today, sociologists tend to accept the concept of role, developed by Znaniecki and Moreno as the smallest unit in the analysis of the social system. Parsons in his three analytical systems identifies different units, depending upon the system: for the social system the term is 'role expectation,' for the cultural system 'value-orientation,' and finally for the personality system, 'need-disposition.' [27]

As far as the extensiveness of the units is concerned, it should be noted that as a result of increasing specialization, sociology today can be conveniently divided into two major subfields, i.e., microsociology and macrosociology, or more colloquially called sociology of small groups, and sociology of the total society as termed by M. Mauss, or comprehensive social processes, as termed by Loomis.[28] While it appears that such a differentiation has not been carried out in the anthropological discipline, there can be found within one sociological department scholars who focus their attention in one of these two directions. Not without interest is the fact that the Harvard group, which has so significantly contributed to the development of the concept of social system, also includes George C. Homans and Fred Bales who have made the concept of social system at home in small group studies. Though Homans in his recent work has dropped the concept of system, his earlier work identified three parts, i.e., action, inter-action, and sentiments, (terms that are considerably closer to phenomenal reality than Parsonian concepts).[29] For Bales the major part is one action unit, classified in his well-known twelve categories organized around the proaction and reaction axis, as well as the reward and punishment axis.[30] Special reference is made to these small group theories of social system here because they provide a certain link and inspiration to a theory of recurrent behavior. Both Homans and Bales deal with repetitive behaviors. Homans' well-known propositions about liking and disliking and the frequency of interaction, contrary to Parsons, take into ac-count the differential recurrence aspect in interaction or action. Bales pioneered by counting frequencies of particular interac-tions, and succeeded in "unfolding" the concept of social group, which had earlier given us a rather static connotation, as a process characterized by different rates and over a period changing re-currences of particular behaviors. One could consequently postu-late that a similar attempt should be made as far as the total society is concerned.

Modus of the Transaction-relationship:

This dimension being strategic for our theory of recurrent behaviors, requires an additional elaboration. A usual procedure at this point would be to suggest that whether a phenomenon should be treated in terms of a causal or telic category or as a part-member of a universal or particular class of phenomena, is a decision to be made by the researcher himself. Since we seek however to develop a phenomenal framework of recurrent be-haviors, our primary commitment is to develop such dimensions as they are experienced by persons who produce recurrent behav-iors. The difference between this action theory as compared to that of Parsons and his co-workers, is that our dimensions are phenomenal and not analytical as far as personal interaction is concerned. This means that these dimensions are directly perceived and experienced by actors in a way similar to "a psychological distance" being perceived by a person in Lewin's topological space. Only in Chapter V where also societal and not only personal recurrences are discussed, will the phenomenal frame of reference be enriched by an analytical one.

Turning to a short survey of the major available theories of social structure and social system in terms of the transaction relationship, let us consider the time dimension first. By definition, past or future are irrelevant here. If parts are interlocked with each other to different degrees, the nexus of the interrelationship is in "the present." Only non-recurrence is a "pure past."

While the time dimension has been disposed of by definition of the recurrent properties of structures and systems, the space dimension creates greater difficulties. At this point a reference should be made to Vilfredo Pareto whose contribution to the development of the concept of social system is of major importance. Historically Pareto can be considered to be the first to introduce the concept not as a taxonomy but as a functional interrelationship, considered by Henderson as Pareto's major contribution.[31] Transferred from economic theory, the notion of mutually dependent variables was certainly a novum in sociology at that time. Elements of the system could be, according to Pareto, anything, but in the social system these were persons with differential degrees of sentiments.[32] It should be noted that contrary to most of his followers, Pareto was thinking also in terms of change. "When, therefore, we speak of the 'social system' we mean that system taken both at a specified moment and in the successive transformations which it undergoes within a specified period of time."[33] Thus Pareto assumed that all parts are related to each other, in a manner later expressed also by Radcliffe-Brown in whose mind social structure covered all existing relations.

Stimulated by Lévi Strauss, Nadel proposed that social structure could be profitably defined as a "statistical model."[34] It means that there is a recurrence only for the majority of parts but not necessarily for all. Robin M. Williams, Jr., has called such a regular failure to comply "patterned evasion." [35] However, if a majority does not comply, then the non-compliance becomes structure if repeated over time. Finally, let us note that Sorokin's concept of cultural system also applies only to a part of the social space. Sorokin refers to major cultural products as being parts of the system. (See in Chapter II). All other items are classified as congeries, which make up in fact a residual category.

It should be noted that the space here involves parts taken more or less from the same level of phenomenal reality. As discussed earlier in reference to possible variations in time extensiveness, there can be not only different space extensiveness of parts but also different levels of phenomenal reality from which the parts are taken. It appears that the concept of social structure especially lends itself to such a free locking of different levels. Georges Gurvitch illustrates an extreme example by listing ten layers which make up a social structure. They form together a precarious equilibrium that must be permanently renewed through new efforts; the layers consist of forms of socialability, social rules, temporalities, mentalities, modes of division of labor and accumulation, functional groups, social classes and their organizations, models and signs and symbols, social roles and finally values and ideas. "In short, these are cultural products that correspond to these structures, or if they are global, to the whole civilization. The latter transcends them and they participate in it both as contributors and benefactors." [36] Gurvitch's structure is an hierarchic concept, involving transactions that could best be described by the term interpenetration. Compared to the usual definition of social system as an order of social roles, it appears that Gurvitch's structure is more comprehensive but also more, and almost alarmingly overlapping.

Thus, we have found two areas to which the concept of space could be applied; first, there is the number of parts involved. We can by definition say that structure as a spatial concept must involve at least a majority of parts. A unique part is, by definition, excluded from the concept of structure or system similarly as the past is excluded.

The second problem, certainly the more difficult and less clarified, is the problem of levels of phenomenal reality. Generally, we assume that the system will cover parts derived from the same level while the notion of structure, less definite on this point, should lend itself better to a linking of different levels.

Degree of Recurrence or Its Absence:

On the basis of our prior definition of structure and social system, it appears at first sight that the above subtitle is in contradiction to whatever has been said so far about these two concepts; nevertheless, students have also sought to accommodate change within the structure concept. Recently in the United States, Murdock and Vogt criticized the structure concept. Murdock, who earlier had been one of the major proponents and developers of the concept, suggested abandoning it altogether because "the static view of social structure . . . seeks explanations exclusively within the existing framework of social system on the highly dubious assumption of cultural stability. . . ."[37] Vogt, although not expressing strong criticism, demanded that observation should be extended over, for example, a period of twenty years.[38]

As far as the system is concerned, Parsons was notoriously criticized for providing a completely static picture of society. Answering his critics, Parsons emphasized a need for developing first a "categorical system" on the basis of which later a change could be erected.[39] If one remembers Pareto's definition of system as well as Parsons' provision for ordered change, it appears that the concept of system would lend itself better to comprehension of change than social structure. Sorokin's super-systems of civilization certainly provide for permanent change, which imply, in Hegelian terms, change as inherent in the system itself.

In view of our major focus on recurrent behaviors, no further discussion of non-recurrences, i.e., the social change concept, is necessary. Interestingly enough, social theory has not yet provided any satisfactory answer as to the continuity and change problem. If Malinowski, for example, defines social system as a succession of activities or events as opposed to a set of abstractions, we are not yet clear whether or how much recurrence or innovation is involved.[40] If some parts change and others recur, under what conditions may we still consider the whole structure the same or different? Evidently, we are meeting a limit of the concept of recurrence that will also be discussed in the following section.

Concept of Recurrence:

As the title of this work suggests, the concept of recurrence is the major concept of our system. In order to discuss it within the time-space framework, it will be necessary to introduce the concept of the number of items as well as the concept of the density of intervals.

We assume that a phenomenon is made up of certain items that can be more or less differentiated. Studies on blind persons who became able to see as a result of eye surgery, indicate that persons who see for the first time, see chaos.[41] Our ordered world is learned through later experience. Certainly, hypotheses of Sapir and even in a more radical way of Whorf on the linguistic determination of our perception, give some evidence that will require more testing.[42] For our purpose here, let us start with the fact that persons perceive the world in certain orders that are more or less stable and circumscribed. Compared to Locke's, and other authors' differentiation between primary and secondary qualities of objects, social action and interaction in which we are primarily interested, could better be differentiated in terms of one-layer present and two-layers past-present, or future-present units as discussed in Chapter I. Thus a phenomenon has not only an extensiveness in space but also in time. Theoretically, since each phenomenon is composed of items, there are n items in time and n items in space that make up the phenomenon. A stable and undifferentiated phenomenon has of course no items with the exception of one space item and one time item.

Since we have here both time and space dimensions and since recurrence is a time dimension phenomenon by definition, one may wonder why the spatial dimension should also be relevant. The reason is that by means of the shifting level of abstraction, i.e., by eliminating a certain number of items, the recurrence can be still maintained, although some items were dropped or added. The problem remains, of course, of how many items can be changed in a phenomenon so that the phenomenon would still recur although somewhat changed. A recurrence could be defined in terms of identity but such a definition would be very strict. If we relax the criterion of identity, changing it into that of similarity, we seem to be closer to the world of experience. After all, there is no total identity in the phenomenal world because a phenomenon changes at least in its time property, i.e., it is becoming "older." A complete identity would require a constant elimination of the memory, a postulate of physical science but not of social science.

The concept of similarity is certainly more viable than identity but it is not a logical concept.[43] Logically one could only say that if a phenomenon retains 51% of its items and 49% are changed, this is still a recurrent, i.e., similar phenomenon. Behaviorally, such a formula can work only with difficulty, depending upon the threshold of discrimination of items and other factors. But the concept of similarity can be improved if we introduce the concept of interval density, already listed in prior sections.

The interval density is based upon memory and upon our span of perceiving items as one phenomenon. However instead of dealing with the time during which the phenomenon is extended, we are interested in its opposite, i.e., the time during which the phenomenon is interrupted, namely the interval. From that it follows, by definition, that when the interval density approaches zero, the phenomenon tends to exist almost without any cessation. On the other hand when the interval density approaches 1, the phenomenon occurs rarely, and if there is 1, the phenomenon does not occur at all. The interval density that approaches zero is also a measure for an increasing intensity of the phenomenon in regard to the observer. If a phenomenon is "intensive," if a person is "ego-involved" speaking in M. Sherif's term, there are few if any intervals.[44] Under more average conditions, the phenomenon is frequently suspended because of new phenomena invading the span of attention.[45]

Thus we have here an ongoing competition among different phenomena and images for a person's attention. Which among these are recurrent behaviors? It appears that recurrent behaviors are those phenomena or images which have a high interval density. For recurrent behaviors are usually only partially admitted to the threshold of our attention, and in that sense they are not intensive. The phenomenon and its situation are structured. When they are unstructured, this would promote organizatory tendencies on the part of the subject, and in that sense not any more recurrent but innovatory behaviors, as pointed out by Kastenbaum.[46]

The above surprising result is likely to be improved if we introduce a new term, i.e., familiarity. Thus recurrent behavior is a familar behavior that absorbs only marginally our attention, or which absorbs our attention only temporarily to be relegated speedily to our memory. Moreover, in the memory after a few recurrences the date of the particular recurrence tends to be erased. Considered from this viewpoint, the recurrent behavior appears to be on the borderline of habits. However, the recurrent behavior is not an habitual behavior if the latter is understood to be performed with a high degree of the density interval. Recurrent behavior is a behavior that persons are aware of but whose particular recollection is dissolved within a series of recurrent behaviors that are not differentiated but amalgamated within one series. The recurrent behavior stands between habit and innovatory behaviors. The latter becomes a recurrent behavior as soon as it is repeated.

In the next chapter a theory of personality will be introduced in terms of recurrent and innovatory behaviors. In the following sections, an examination of the recurrent behavior, from now on identified as RB, will be undertaken in categories of the existential locus, parts, and finally the modus of transaction-relationship.

Existential Locus of RB:

The reader has probably noticed by now that contrary to a sociological or anthropological approach the approach here has utilized predominantly psychological concepts. The approach thus far has been in terms of the individual's perception of time and space. However, this is only a methodological characteristic of the presentation, i.e., to start with the smallest unit and gradually expand the recurrence concept to the group and interpersonal and institutional-societal frame of reference.

Consequently, there will be differentiated in the following chapter two loci of recurrent behaviors: first, there is the perception of the actor himself. This is a classification of his as well as other persons' behaviors as RB or IB (innovatory behavior). It is also his level of abstraction on which he extends a particular present, respectively images of future or past.

Secondly, there is the locus of the actor's behavior being classified as a RB or IB by other persons around him, i.e., other actors. If other actors are able to predict what the actor is likely to do within his daily and other temporal cycles, his behavior is then classified as RB from the group viewpoint, otherwise IB from the group viewpoint. Thus, we should differentiate between two types of RB, i.e., individual and group, and two types of IB, individual and group. What implications derived therefrom (i.e., if there is no convergence between these individual and group classifications) will be examined in following chapters.

There will be as little as possible usage of the analyst's locus in the study of RB and IB. As defined earlier, recurrence is a phenomenon perceived by the actors themselves and not by analysts. Were it the latter, the discussion would expand into an almost infinite number of possible categories of recurrences.

It should be remembered that RB does not cover only social relations as defined, for example, by Weber or Parsons and others, but *all* perceived RB from the individual as well as group viewpoints. Of course, the primary focus here is upon social interactions. The enlargement of RB by including non-interactional phenomena is not unusual, as indicated by Homans' earlier system in which actions as well as interactions are included.

Parts and Extensiveness of RB:

In order to avoid terminological vagueness, it would be well at this point to introduce specific definitions. This is especially a requisite here, since many authors, as noted earlier, use different terms when discussing the whole-part relationship in social phenomena. Moreover, the reader has probably noted in the above section on RB, that a new term, "item," was introduced. One could ask why not use the term "part" consistently instead of the term "item"? Or even better, why not accept the mathematical convention and speak all through the text of sets and elements?

First, the term "item" refers to the differentiable quality or property of a phenomenon or an image. Despite the Gestalt emphasis upon wholes in human perception, wholes are differentiable into smaller items, as students of perception have not failed to point out.[47] Though terms such as "property," "attribute" or "quale" could be used, it appears that the term "item" has been less "loaded" with different connotations, and therefore is more desirable. Thus any phenomenon has at least two items, i.e., space and time dimensions. As far as an image is concerned, the space or time reference can but need not always be present. RB, for example, tends to eliminate the temporal date item. Most phenomena have of course a greater number of items than only the spatial and temporal items. Most images have also more items though they tend more to omit than add items when compared to phenomena.

When speaking about phenomena or images we have made a somewhat strong assumption that they naturally appear as differentiable entities, or as sometimes called "perceptual units" that are characterized by "perceptual invariance." [48] Since the human mind not only accepts those "givens" but also carves out and imposes its own boundaries upon the phenomenal world, we have introduced concepts of part, unit, structure and system. These concepts refer to a more abstract level of relations. Thus when a phenomenon is conceived of along a time dimension that transcends its own present, we have temporal units. We remember that time units can change with levels of abstraction. When a phenomenon is conceived of more in its present relational structure with other phenomena, we have a part. Analogically, there are temporal and spatial structures. Also, when boundaries are quite pronounced and the structure is able to transact in a unified manner, we have temporal and spatial systems. One can wonder why a differentiation between temporal and spatial is pursued here when clearly no phenomenon can be only temporal or spatial. If one recalls that he deals not only with phenomena but also images, the differentiation is justified.

Another problem, of course, is the notion of boundaries of a phenomenon. It is interesting to note that Barker and his co-workers on the basis of empirical data have found that most persons organized natural units in terms of goal-directed acts.[49] Barker and associates obtained their data by exposing subjects to a present-bound stimulus. It can be assumed that even more meaningful "natural units" could be obtained if persons were asked to report what they had been doing some time ago. One property of RB, as defined above, is that the date disappears and only the dateless unit or structures remain. For example, one forgets what one ate for breakfast seven days ago but one is confident in reporting that within a particular span of time in the morning one consumed a breakfast seven days ago. Unfortunately there has been extremely little done on RB empirically. My own research in a Polish factory disclosed that workers did not remember how their work output went a few days ago. All they remembered was that they worked. In that sense work was a RB without any items as such, if reported in terms of memory

data. Of course, if given direct attention, there would be a
number of items that could be differentiated. Memory however
simplifies even when we turn around and try to imagine an
object just seen, as shown for example by Ames in his discussion
of so-called ultrastimulus perception.[50]

Thus we are led to the conclusion that RB is differentiated
best on the basis of memory referring to past activities or interactions. The individual definition of RB should converge with
the group definition that is based upon a prediction by other
members of the group of what the person has done or is likely
to do in the future. If there is considerable agreement between
the past references and the future references for both the individual and the group, we can conclude that these are the chains of
RB most frequently differentiated.

The result of our discussion then is that we prefer to define
RB in terms of the past or future behaviors and not in terms
of direct attention to the present behavior. The reason for this
transcending of the present situation is that the present behavior
as such is not yet the recurrent behavior. The recurrence is
obtained only over a period. Since recurrence is not an analyst's
notion but an experience of the actor and group, it must be
defined in terms of the actor's images of past and future behaviors.

In concluding this section, it should be pointed out that we
assume an individual person has a whole repertoire of chains
of RB. It is an individual chain if made up of temporal units of
RB; however, when one chain is related to another chain, i.e.,
when we start looking at phenomena in terms of the present, we
speak of spatial parts. One of the exciting problems from the
theoretical point of view is to explore possibilities of how a time
units structure is ralated to the spatial parts structure.

Modus of the Transaction-Relationship of RB:

Turning now to the problem of degree of interrelationship
between spatial parts and temporal units, there will be utilized
the concept of interval density. Let us assume that both time

and space dimensions can be related to each other as coordinates whose axes are stretched along the interval density. Remember that the maximum degree of transaction is at the zero point, i.e., in the following figure the point at the origin.

Figure 1
TIME AND SPACE DIMENSIONS AND INTERVAL DENSITIES

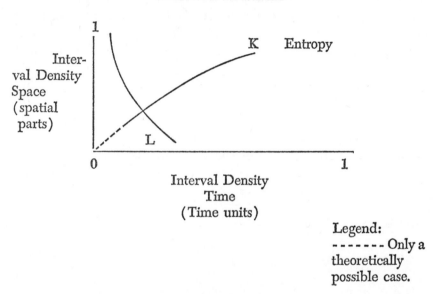

Legend:
------- Only a theoretically possible case.

In the above figure curve L indicates that there is a reverse relation between time units and spatial parts if measured in the density intervals. Curve K on the contrary shows there is a positive relationship between time units and spatial parts.[51] As function K approaches the origin, the degree of interrelationship between time units and spatial parts increases, ultimately being only a theoretically possible case. As function K moves away from the origin, the interdependence decreases, the system or structure becomes looser, and eventually completely dissolves. Speaking in physical terms, there would be maximum entropy.

When function is close to the origin, i.e., when units of one
RB chain are maximally bound to each other, there is a maximum
independence from other chains. This would be illustrated by
highly autonomous activities such as physiological processes
and mental processes. Interestingly, the more adult and socialized
a person is, the more he can segregate particular processes and
activities from each other, and simultaneously the more he becomes involved in different social roles that make him more
dependent. It appears that the autonomy one achieves in one
realm of his life is paid or compensated for by becoming more
dependent in other realms. This is in fact what function L
says: if each of the chains of RB are strongly linked in their
time units structure, there will be little variation in their time
spatial parts structure. The parts will remain autonomous, and
they will coexist without relating too much to each other. It appears that the concept of the social system as developed by
modern sociologists tends to emphasize the part structure of
phenomena at the expense of the temporal structure. How these
temporal and spatial structures are related to each other, will be
the problem of the next two chapters.

NOTES

1. Talcott Parsons, *The Social System* (Glencoe, Ill.: The Free Press,
1951), p. 39.
2. Marion J. Levy, Jr., *The Structure of Society* (Princeton: Princeton
University Press, 1952), p. 58.
3. Raymond Firth, "Some Principles of Social Organisation," *Journal of
Royal Anthropological Institute of Great Britain and Ireland*, Parts I and II,
(85) January–December 1955, p. 2.
4. S. F. Nadel, *The Theory of Social Structure* (Glencoe, Ill.: The Free
Press, 1958), pp. 8–11.
5. Gabriel Tarde, *The Laws of Imitation* (New York: Holt 1903). See
especially the discussion of imitation on pp. 74–207.
6. Henry Pratt Fairchild, ed., *Dictionary of Sociology* (New York:
Philosophical Library; 1944), p. 310 and 315.

7. Charles Winick, *Dictionary of Anthropology* (Ames, Iowa: Little-field-Adams, 1958), p. 313.

8. Meyer Fortes, *The Web of Kinship Among the Tallensi* (London: Oxford University Press for Internatl. African Institute, 1949), p. 342.

9. Lewis H. Morgan, *Systems of Consanguinity and Affinity* (Washington, D.C.: Smithsonian Institute, 1870) Vol. XVII of Smithsonian Contributions to Knowledge.

10. See Lévi–Strauss commentary in Roger Bastide, ed., *Sens et Usage Terme Structure dans les Sciences Humaines et Sociales*, Janua Linguarum Nu XVI, ('S-Gravenhage, Mouton 1962), p. 143.

11. Firth, *op. cit.*, p. 15.

12. Nadel, *op. cit.*, p. 151.

13. Charles P. Loomis, *Social Systems: Essays on Their Persistence and Change* (Princeton, New Jersey: D. Van Nostrand, 1960), p. 3.

14. See Parsons' "An Outline of the Social System," in Talcott Parsons *et. al. Theories of Society: Foundations of Modern Sociological Theory.* Vol. 1 (Glencoe, Ill.: The Free Press, 1961), p. 36.

15. *Ibid.*, p. 36.

16. Bastide, *op. cit.*, p. 152.

17. Ludwig von Bertalanffy, "General System Theory: A Critical Review," *General Systems* (VII) 1962, pp. 1–20.

18. Bastide, *op. cit.*, p. 153.

19. E. R. Leach, *Political Systems of Highland Burma: A Study of Kachin Social Structure* (Boston: Beacon Press, 1964), pp. 1–17. For a critique of Leach's approach see also Ernest Gellner, "Time and Theory in Social Anthropology," *Mind*, (67) 1958, pp. 182–202.

20. Claude Lévi-Strauss, *Structural Anthropology* (New York: Basic Books, 1963), p. 279.

21. Bastide, *op. cit.*, p. 145.

22. Nadel, *op. cit.*, p. 150.

23. Talcott Parsons and Edward A. Shils, eds., *Toward a General Theory of Action* (Cambridge, Mass.: Harvard University Press, 1952), p. 237–240, p. 39, p. 55. Later, the notion of culture as an abstract system was enlarged: culture is a behavior system as well as an abstract system, depending upon the approach. See A. L. Kroeber and Talcott Parsons "The Concepts of Culture and Social System," *American Sociological Review*, (23) October 1958, pp. 582–583. See also more recent Parsons et al., *Theories of Society*, Vol. II, *op. cit.*, p. 964.

24. See Sol Tax *et al.*, eds., *An Appraisal of Anthropology Today* (Chicago: University of Chicago Press, 1953), pp. 299–321.

25. For different definitions see Nadel, *op. cit.*, p. 5. Also Dorothy Emmet, "How Far Can Structural Studies Take Account of Individuals," *The Jour-*

nal of Royal Anthropological Institute of Great Britain and Ireland, Part I,
(90) July-December 1960, pp. 191–200. Also Raymond Firth, "Social Organisation and Social Change," *Journal of Royal Anthropological Institute of
Great Britain and Ireland,* Part I and II (84), January-December 1954,
pp. 1–20.

26. P. A. Sorokin, *Society, Culture and Personality: Their Structure and
Dynamics* (New York: Harper, 1947), p. 39.

27. Parsons and Shils, *op. cit.,* p. 235.

28. Marcel Mauss, *Sociologie et Anthropologie* (Paris: Presses Universitaires de France, 1950), pp. 274–5.

29. George C. Homans, *The Human Group* (New York: Harcourt, Brace,
1950), pp. 33–40, 80–155 and *Social Behavior: Its Elementary Forms*
(New York: Harcourt, Brace, 1961), pp. 51–82.

30. Robert F. Bales, *Interaction Analysis* (Reading, Mass.: Addison-
Wesley, 1951). See also a discussion of Bales' system in John Madge, *The
Origins of Scientific Sociology* (Glencoe, Ill.: The Free Press, 1962), pp.
424–471.

31. Lawrence J. Henderson, *Pareto's General Sociology: A Physiologist's
Interpretation* (Cambridge: Harvard University Press, 1935), p. 16.

32. *Ibid.,* p. 30.

33. Vilfredo Pareto, *The Mind and Society* (New York: Harcourt Brace,
1935), Vol. IV, p. 1435.

34. Nadel, *op. cit.,* p. 147.

35. Robin M. Williams, Jr., *American Society: A Sociological Interpretation* (New York: A. A. Knopf, 1952), Chapt. 10.

36. Bastide, *op. cit.,* p. 153.

37. George P. Murdock, "Changing Emphasis in Social Structure,"
Southwestern Journal of Anthropology (11) No. 4, 1955, p. 366.

38. Evon Z. Vogt, "On the Concept of Structure and Process in Cultural Anthropology," *American Anthropologist* (62) No. 1, 1960, p. 29.

39. Parsons and Shils, *op. cit.,* pp. 50–51.

40. Referred to by E. E. Evans-Pritchard, *Social Anthropology* (London:
Cohen and West, 1951), p. 94.

41. See M. von Senden, *Space and Sight: The Perception of Space and
Shape in the Congenitally Blind Before and After Operation* (London: Peter
Heath, 1960).

42. For a discussion of Sapir and Whorf's theories see Harry Hoijer "The
Relation of Language to Culture," in A. L. Kroeber, ed., *Anthropology Today: An Encyclopedic Inventory* (Chicago: University of Chicago Press,
1953).

43. See Kant's discussion of these two categories defined as "a regulative
principle" in *Immanuel Kant's Critique of Pure Reason* (London: Macmillan,

1933), pp. 537–549. In order that two phenomena should be differentiated as "different," at least one of their properties must not be the same. See George A. Kelly, *The Psychology of Personal Constructs*, (New York: Norton, 1955), pp. 242–308.

44. M. Sherif and Carolyn W. Sherif, *An Outline of Social Psychology* (New York: Harper, 1956), pp. 579–615.

45. It should be noticed that so far the concept of phenomenon has been used in its largest possible connotation. An image retained in the mind from a psychological viewpoint is also a phenomenon. From now on, however, since we are concerned with time and space dimension, the term "phenomenon" will be restricted only to objects "or processes outside the head." G. Bachelard uses a suggestive concept in reference to time intervals, i.e., "lacuna." See Gaston Bachelard, *La Dialectique de la Durée* (Paris: Boivin, 1936), p. 92.

46. Robert Kastenbaum, "The Dimensions of Future Time Perspective: An Experimental Analysis," *Journal of General Psychology*, (65) 1961, pp. 203–218.

47. See for a general orientation William H. Ittelson, *Visual Space Perception* (New York, Springer, 1960) or William N. Dember, *The Psychology of Perception* (New York: Holt, 1961).

48. See Leonard S. Cottrell, Jr., "The Analysis of Situational Fields in Social Psychology," *American Sociological Review* (7) 1942, pp. 370–382. For the term "perceptual invariance," see Ittelson, *op. cit.*, p. 54.

49. Harold R. Dickman, "The Perception of Behavioral Units," pp. 39–40 in Roger B. Barker, ed., *The Stream of Behavior: Explorations of Its Structure and Content* (New York: Appleton-Century-Crofts, 1963).

50. Adelbert Ames, Jr., "Ultra-Stimulus Perception," p. 309 in Franklin P. Kilpatrick, *Explorations in Transactional Psychology* (New York: New York University Press, 1961).

51. An example of a positive relationship between both dimensions is provided by studies on estimates of spatial and temporal lengths. See, for example, John Cohen and Peter Cooper and Akio Ono. "The Hare and the Tortoise: A Study of the Tau-effect in Walking and Running," *Acta Psychologica* (Amsterdam) (21) 1963, pp. 387–393.

IV PERSONAL RB AND GROUP RB

In this chapter both personal and group RB, as defined earlier, will be developed as chains of RB. The difference between behavioral and image RB will also be discussed. Thus, there will be differentiation between behavioral RB and image RB as well as personal and group categories of RB. Altogether four different categories of RB will be considered. Also concepts of three different spaces—physical, social and cultural—will be discussed.

Before we start the presentation, an introductory comment on the temporal and spatial dimensions as related to personal and group RB is in order. As defined earlier, the group RB is such that a group predicts or reports RB of a person. To be sure, it is not an aggregate of individual RB or a collective RB. This problem of aggregate RB and collective RB will be discussed in the next chapter.

Though the focus in this chapter still predominantly rests upon one single person, either as perceived by himself, or by the group, there nevertheless appears a tendency for the personal RB to be more projected along the time dimension as compared to the group RB. Though the group RB is also a temporal unit, it is also, to some degree, a spatial part. This is due simply to the fact about the existential locus that reference to another person's behavior involves a spatial relationship, i.e., the relation between the observer and the person. Of course, one should note that physical space is not involved as much as social space in this instance.

Personal Behavioral RB:

Again, there are definitions to be clarified at the outset of this section. The concept of interval density calls for further differentiation. As developed earlier, the concept did not distinguish between intervals occurring within one phenomenal stretch and between several such stretches. It should be noted that RB to which present attention is given is in fact, according to the earlier definition of RB, full of short intervals; one could say that the RB is porous. A high porosity, like a high interval density, would move RB closer to a habit. However the porosity is not applicable in regard to the image RB, as will be shown below.

Turning to intervals, two additional items can be differentiated, namely duration of the interval and the frequency of the intervals. In the theory of RB the latter term is especially relevant. As stated earlier, the differential frequency of particular chains of RB has not been explored yet, with the exception of Durkheim's observation on religious rituals.

The concept of chain of RB already has been used, and is self-explanatory. A question of "how many chains" can be differentiated cannot, at least at present, be answered. There are, of course, ethnographic and other classifications of human behaviors, more or less organized as taxonomies. There are unstructured observations by Barker,[1] as well as a classificatory scheme for a stream of behavior developed by Marvin Harris.[2] Practically all time budget studies deal with the problem of identification of categories of activities, i.e., chains of RB. Sorokin and Berger, for example, let respondents record their activities in an unstructured way, later analytically subsuming their responses into 55 different categories.[3] In an American study of 1954, all activities were first classified as "at home" or "away at home"; the former was analytically broken down into 6 categories, the latter into 7 categories.[4] Another American 1957 study used 21 categories.[5] It is noteworthy that in both these studies different methods were used. In the 1954 studies persons recorded their activities every 15 minutes on a log sheet, while in the 1957 study persons were interviewed after one day. Thus the latter comes close to our former definition of RB as an activity that transcends present behavior.

It is appropriate here to refer briefly to some European studies that have recently been concerned with two major categories, i.e., work and leisure activities. Under Dumazedier's leadership a major cross-cultural study of workers' leisure involving six European countries used six categories.[6] Like an American study by Ross and Bostian a Czechoslovak study used only two categories, work and nonwork.[7] Soviet sociologists who have in recent years initiated their sociological research primarily in the field of time budget studies, generally use more categories, mainly concentrating, however, on work and related activities.[8] of the three variables.

One problem that appears in connection with the establishment of categories within which chains of RB could be classified, is the problem of simultaneous activities, e.g., eating and reading the newspaper.[9] This multiple character of human activities tends to be solved if the RB is studied *post factum*. Less significant or incidental activities tend to be forgotten, or are not anticipated.

Probability of Recurrence:

Provided that a list of chains of RB's is collected as reported by a person, we can introduce another consideration, namely the probability with which an RB would be in fact recurring within a specific time span. Probability will be defined here in terms of past frequencies.[10] Suppose sleep is treated as one chain. It is fairly clear that sleep is a rather high probability chain. In a Hungarian study of the time budget of employed persons, according to Szalai, there is very little variation in the time allocated to sleep even when other activities had to be substantially cut down or eventually eliminated because of some increasing new time demands.[11] Thus, we can assume that, generally, there will be a high probability for RB that are biologically derived. One could consequently rank all chains of RB according to the degree of probability of their recurrences. It is likely that most persons would tend to have similar probabilities in regard to biologically derived RB, if the persons were categorized according to age and sex. Personality and social role differences would appear in regard to probabilities of non-biologically derived RB which, presumably, would not have such great probabilities as biological RB. The following figure illustrates the above discussion.

Figure 2

CHAINS OF RECURRENT BEHAVIORS OF ONE PERSON RANKED ACCORDING TO PROBABILITY OF RECURRENCE

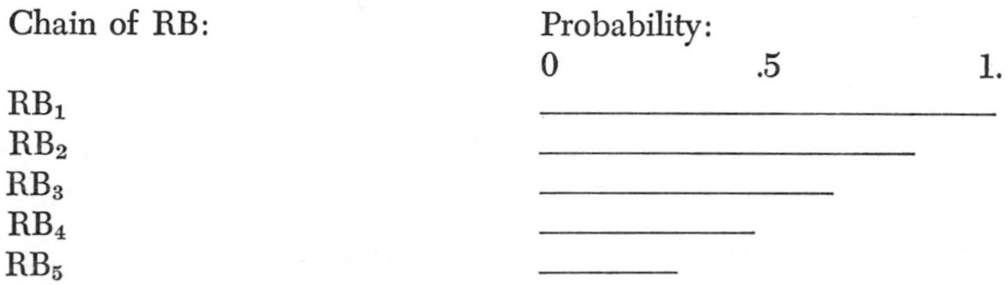

Chain of RB: Probability:

	0	.5	1.
RB_1			
RB_2			
RB_3			
RB_4			
RB_5			

It should be noted that by introducing the concept of probability of RB we have in fact enlarged our former scheme that defined RB primarily in terms of their interval densities, or more specifically in terms of interval frequency and interval duration. It is clear that likewise we can speak of RB frequency and RB duration. From now on both RB and interval dimensions will be used. It should be noticed that the concept of interval is applicable to only one particular chain of RB. The interval thus exists in regard to the particular RB only, being "filled out" either by other RB chains, or by an IB (innovatory behavior). Therefore, in the above figure the complement of the probability of a particular chain, i.e., the probability that the particular RB will *not recur*, is "filled out" by all other chains as well as IB. Recalling the definition of IB, one must maintain the IB cannot form chains. According to the Markov chain theory, an IB, when it has been repeated, becomes "absorbed" into a new RB.[12] In general, it is probable that those RB with low probability are

likely to disappear eventually, and that many IB which become
RB, maintain themselves only for a certain span of time and
also tend to recede after some recurrent runs. From this it follows
that a major personality change occurs only when RB with higher
probabilities are affected. One can almost visualize the higher
probability RB as a structure of a channel within whose flow
emerge and submerge small probability RB as well as IB.

If there are three variables, i.e., the number of RB chains, the
frequency of each RB, and the duration of one RB, there also
can be three different types of probabilities. Certainly, there is
also a number of possible combinations of the three variables.
However, since there are only 24 hours in a day [or 168 hours
in a week, or 8,736 hours in a year], the three variables are
mutually interdependent. Consequently not all three can keep
increasing or decreasing at the same time. So, for example, if
one imposes a restriction that a variable can either increase or
decrease or remain stable, then there are only 13 possible changes
of the three variables.

Which variables are more likely to experience a change? For
most chains of RB, it is quite plausible to propose that there is a
hierarchy at whose top is the number of chains most resistant
to change, i.e., whose recurrence probability is highest. While the
higher RB chains are more invariant, their duration might be
more variable. Generally speaking, an increase in variation of
duration, i.e., the decrease in the duration probability value is
an index for many RB chains that the frequency will be affected.
And if the frequency is affected increasingly, this is an index that
the chain itself experiences a major change. Under such variable
conditions, the chain is losing in its probability value, and drops
down in the probability rank order set of chains. Once it has
become a low probability RB, it is likely to be eventually dropped
completely.

The above statement is alarmingly broad, and calls for further
specification. It appears that a useful differentiation consists again
of biologically-derived and culturally-derived RB. If one considers
the biological RB he is confronted with the fact that they stand

high on recurrence probability. However, if one would apply not only the duration variable but also the being "on a point of time" variable, the biologically derived RB would have low probability. On this criterion many culturally derived work and transportation RB would conversely be very high. Thus while biological RB almost always recur, they do not recur on precise time. After all, note also that two major biological facts such as birth or death in most cases can be predicted only within certain ranges of time, and hardly "on the point of time." The variable of precision is a cultural variable while biologically derived RB appear more diffuse though highly regular in terms of frequencies. Therefore, the above elaboration on a certain hierarchical order of criteria of change that starts most likely with changing duration, then affects frequency and then at last drops the whole chain of RB, is applicable primarily to cultural RB.

The hierarchy of gradual changes should be particularly relevant in more unstructured social groups. If RB are formalized, then a change is likely to occur on all criteria simultaneously. The formalization is thus a normative restriction that occurs among spatial parts as well as temporal units. Speaking more illustratively, a person is expected to speak only to particular persons, and eventually in particular localities. Note that if the spatial dimension follows the normative prescription while the temporal does not, there are not only embarrassments but also humorous situations. A lord and his attendant stranded on a little island and yet following the established time order of their former life are a frequent topic of comics.

Cycles and Patterns:

RB can recur within different time intervals. These temporal differences will be identified by us as levels of cycles. The lower the level, the shorter the cycle, e.g., the 24 hours cycle would be on a lower level than the monthly cycle. Of course, the temporal flow of the present does not differentiate between levels because a low level cycle RB can be followed in the next minute by a high level cycle RB. However, man has developed ability to switch from one cycle to another cycle. In fact, it would be quite appropriate that man, because of his cultural buttressing, can operate several "reference RB cycles." For example, the ability to shift purposively from shorter cycles to longer cycles accounts for a person's ability to sustain stress and failures.[13] By shifting a RB that disappointingly did not appear next day, to a one-week or one-month-cycle, one is enabled to continue his efforts. Moreover by the extending of time cycles, one can reduce tensions and eliminate conflicts. If there is competition within a cultural space for particular items, a transfer to a longer cycle can eliminate the competitive sting, and in fact stretch the dense competitive relationship into a looser one, and within a longer cycle, a less intense relationship. This shift of cycles mechanism, in fact a transcendence, is common to all religions, and not so long ago was reported by Hylan Lewis in his interpretation of Southern Negroes'[14] adjustment to the "tough" dominant white culture.

In addition to cycles and their levels one also can determine several, in fact a continuously large number of patterns of RB. Referring to only one cycle, one sees three major patterns: regular, semi-regular and irregular. The latter becomes regular if the time cycle is changed; otherwise an irregular RB would be nothing more than an IB.

The regular pattern could be represented by the most elementary two-chains pattern such as a b, a b, a b, . . . etc., exemplified by a work- leisure dichotomy of some time budget studies. The a-b pattern is rather uninformative and certainly there could be more chains of RB. There is not an infinite number of chains, however. There cannot even be a great number of chains because the property of recurrence would be lost to actors as well as to participant observers. If there is a great number of chains, there is a greater likelihood that the pattern will not be regular, but only semi-regular.

The semi-regular pattern of RB is a pattern in which some chains return regularly, and some irregularly; however, the irregular returnees also must return unless they should be classified as IB. It goes without saying that the semi-regular pattern is the most common pattern, in fact this is the most adequate pattern to be reported spontaneously by actors or participant observers. It is rather unlikely that most persons would report a regular pattern unless instructed to report their activities in rather general terms such as work and rest.

To exemplify a semi-regular pattern, the following scheme is offered:

$$a\ b\ c\ d\ e\ f,\ a\ b\ d\ e\ c\ f,\ a\ b\ e\ f\ c\ d\ .\ .\ .$$

It is evident that there can be different degrees of regularity, or irregularity. Note that all the above chains are RB, and that naturally the pattern would become more irregular if IB were also included.

The third major pattern is the irregular pattern in which elements would reappear in a random order. It is highly unlikely that such a pattern of RB could exist for most persons participating in social organizations. Moreover, it is also unlikely that without a minimum degree of some ordered recurrence, the person would recognize some RB as members of particular chains, if the number of chains were large. Consider only the fact that with merely six chains, the number of possible patterns—if one allows for irregularity—is 6 i.e., 720.

So far the difference between patterns was due only to the change of their rank within the cycle. Another set of patterns can be conceived of if the number of chains also is changed. This means that in a cycle a chain will not appear but it will reappear at each second or n-th cycle. It must however recur within a time at which it is still remembered, otherwise it would have to be classified as an IB.

Theoretically, the greater the number of levels of cycles, the greater the probability that each chain, however irregular within one cycle, will appear regular within another cycle. The requirement here is only that the level of the cycle be "higher," i.e., the cycle must be "longer." Thus the relationship between levels of cycles is asymmetric and hierarchical. Only the higher level cycles can establish a regularity for lower level cycles, but not vice versa.

The above proposition is important for the theory of complex social organization. Persons occupying higher positions within an organization are persons who ought to be able to see RB within higher cycle levels. Thus an executive is a person who by his position is bound not only to control a larger social space, a greater number of persons, but also a larger social time, i.e., to see RB and the presumed IB as members of higher level cycles.[15] Analogically, a difference between a young person and an experienced adult person is that what the young person considers as IB, for the older person is RB within higher cycles.

On the other hand, a creative person can change a RB into IB by stressing and developing particular items that prevent the RB from being classified as a member of a chain. Contrary to the former process of subsuming behaviors within higher levels of RB cycles, the creative person seeks to individualize behaviors, actualize their uniqueness. A further consideration of this point would bring us to the image personal RB.

Before concluding this section, let us consider once more the multiple cycles scheme. As pointed out earlier, different RB cycles share equally, so to speak, the present flow. Consequently one can differentiate roughly at least two sequences of RB: homogeneous and heterogeneous.

The homogeneous sequence is composed of chains that all recur within more or less the same cycle, say a 24-hour cycle. A heterogeneous sequence is a sequence where chains form together at least a two-cycle sequence. Though this seems plausible, a problem that has not been resolved satisfactorily is to decide where a sequence begins and ends. It appears most convenient to use culturally determined sequences such as days, weeks, and months. If the day sequence is used, one can argue that a work day has a tendency for most persons to be a homogeneous sequence while holidays tend to be heterogeneous. The uniqueness, or we may say with Durkheim, the sacredness of a RB appears to be bound to the heterogeneity of sequences, and to the higher level cycles. By breaking up the homogeneity of chains and by transcending the lower level cycles, special significance is attributed to RB. Certainly birthdays and other anniversaries of personal and family life are based upon the heterogeneity and higher cycles levels. Because of this one also can see why heterogeneity and shifting of levels must be less frequent than homogeneity of sequences. Were it otherwise, an inflationary evaluation would reduce the significance of those particular RB whose "sacredness" has been actualized. Note also that by actualizing and in that sense raising their significance, the RB approaches an IB. To avoid it, one needs a particular abstraction that is probably characteristic of true social and intellectual leaders who have developed a larger social consciousness within which they are able to submerge their individual temporal reference cycles. Within the framework of such a large cycle, for example, the unique IB of individual entry into and exit from life appears then as one of a large class of similar RB. The survival of the individual person then can appear of secondary importance as compared to the survival of the group.[16]

Personal Image RB:

The problem that poses itself at the very outset of this section is of course the problem of operationalizing the concept of the image RB. By definition the personal image RB is a recurrent behavior that is manifested in an absence of any particular overt behavior. It will be identified by RB_i. From the behavioristic viewpoint one can give nothing but a negative definition. It is important to recall that in other fields such a heuristically negative definition is also sometimes used.[17]

The RB_i thus refers to past or future recurrent behaviors. These then would be images of the past, or images of the future. We should not however, confuse these with the two-layers present. The RB_i is distinctly separated from the present, it does not belong to the present.[18] Under certain conditions the RB_i loses its date index, and becomes in general, undated imagery. Certainly, a day-dream whose topic is more or less repeated would fall under the RB_i too. Though we do not have a satisfactory technique for measuring the RB_i at least not at present, the theory of recurrent behaviors has to include them.

What kind of propositions made about RB earlier would also be relevant in regard to RB_i? Though one could postulate as well that there are chains, frequencies and duration and probability variables also involved here, it appears that the RB_i is considerably simpler. Though there can be several chains, they do not compete with each other for attention because they are separated from each other by the present RB or IB. In other words, the significance of RB_i appears in relationship to RB; a good example of a RB_i would be a daily reflection, before sleeping, on chains of RB of the completed day. If such a RB_i is for example coupled also with prayer, it becomes in fact an institutionalized RB_i. Note that institutionalization moves the RB_i closer to RB. Certainly an occupation of a planner or a historian, etc., should not be classified as future RB_i or past RB_i, but as present-bound behavioral RB.

Comparison of RB_i and RB discloses further differences than only that of the relatively simpler structure of the former. Though simpler, the RB_i appears to have less porosity than RB. It is not on the borderline of habit but absorbs all attention because it has to be actively developed and not more or less passively attended. This active characteristic of the RB_i accounts for its importance in the study of human behavior. It absorbs not only a quantity of time flow; but it also nurtures a person's values from which plans will be developed. Note that, like Strauss to whom reference was made in Chapter I, Minkowski also has pointed out that only in some mentally pathological cases are persons unable to develop actively images of the future; if persons are affected mentally, they grasp only the present and the past.[19]

Since RB_i generally make greater demands upon a person's mind than RB, they are also likely to introduce more new items. Thus, as stated earlier, RB_i and especially future RB_i are very close to IB; in fact one can assume that creativity is realized by the *élan* with which RB_i are produced. Items tend to appear within the image stream in new combinations.

The continuous-diffuse relationship between RB_i and IB is complemented by another link. As earlier defined, RB is not only the present attendance of behaviors but involves also a tendency to perceive it as a member of a series-chain. When the cycles of chains are longer, there is a greater tendency to rely upon RB_i. For example, a birthday becomes especially meaningful as an RB when compared to other birthdays. While the time-indexing of RB_i tends to appear in longer cycles, their chains tend to have fewer members. The birthday example provides more individual items for particular RB_i than, for example, RB_i of a breakfast consumed one week ago. In the latter case, most likely there would be nothing but a dateless RB_i.

The above analysis leads then to the following conclusion: the more frequent RB is, the less it will be remembered with a date as RB_i. The less frequent RB is, the more likely it will be remembered as RB_i. The date is, of course, an individualizing item. In that sense RB_i approaches IB.

Consider the probability of RB_i. Generally speaking, unless there is some sort of institutionalization, the probability of RB_i is low. Though RB_i are related to RB, mostly they do not appear with any observable regularity; in fact, unless institutionalized, RB_i cannot have a great probability; and yet they recur in forms of future plans or memories of past rewarding actions. Their pattern is hardly regular. It is not amazing that we possess practically no empirical data on RB_i and yet these are a hotbed of IB.

Group Behavioral RB: Physical, Social, and Cultural Spaces:

References to the term "space" have appeared somewhat generously throughout the previous pages. At this point, it is necessary to distinguish between three notions of space, i.e., physical space, social space and cultural space. The social space here means the number of persons or organizations involved. The cultural space means the number of cultural items that are available in regard to a particular problem. Since, for example, a decision is a conceptual process, the items refer primarily to "nonmaterial culture." An innovation then contributes to the cultural space. If there are no items available, and if the problem remains unstructured, one would speak about a small or zero cultural space. Thus the dimension of the cultural space is simply given by the number of cultural items that can be identified as relevant to a particular issue, or issues. The latter also could be counted as well as the number of more general concepts under which the issues could be subsumed. Theoretically, one should regressively come to a unity, the great summit of many philosophical and religious systems.

The above definitions, suggested occasionally in earlier chapters, require additional comments. First, note that the cultural space is not defined in terms of a pattern or organization of meanings, etc., as conceived of by Sorokin. In the mind, the space is not organized, but cultural items in cultural space tend to develop structures. While Sorokin stresses the non-quantitative aspect of his cultural space, the emphasis here upon the number of items available makes the quantitative aspect quite pronounced. In this respect our notion differs also from Lewin's hodological space with which it shares the concept of differentiation. However, Lewin's increasing differentiation or de-differentiation implies the quantitative aspect. Finally, an acknowledgment of Deutsch' influence should be recorded here. The cultural space is then conceived of as a stored number of items available for usage. If this is the case, then, since persons are not computers, the retrieval of cultural space items is also significantly a function of time. It takes time, generally speaking, to examine certain alternatives that are available, or to differentiate properly all items. A theory of decision-making conceived as a process in time would have to specify of course conditions under which the above broad proposition would have to be qualified.

Returning now to group behavioral RB, it should be noticed that all three spaces can be relevant in the determination of RB, either as a prediction or a report on past experiences in regard to a particular chain of RB.

For our purpose, let us assume that persons are producing their statements concerning RB individually, without any influence or consultation with other persons of the group. In that case, no immediate group influence enters into the picture. There is only a summation of individual statements as in polls. Therefore the degree of summarized similarities (called "summarized consensus" here) in regard to RB is relevant.

Summarized Consensus:

To explain the degree of the summarized consensus that can be by definition either one or zero (if each person offers a different description of RB) calls for a reference to social and cultural space. Since persons not only coexist as bodies in space but also are related to each other if they form groups, the consensus (from now on the summarized consensus will be so termed) is also a social space concept. If the consensus is great, i.e., if more persons are agreed, the social space is great too. However, if the cultural space shows homogeneity, the number of items should be relatively small and the cultural space should be small. The dimensions of both spaces, social and cultural run, so to speak, in opposite directions. This contradictory tendency of both spaces is very important because it justifies the conceptual differentiation. If both spaces would merely interpenetrate, as maintained by Parsons,[20] or if the social system would be just a subsystem of the cultural system as maintained by Znaniecki,[21] the differentiation between both concepts would be unsatisfactory. After all, discussions have been going on for a long time seeking to elucidate the difference between both concepts. The difference must be based on a contradiction, and not merely partial overlapping.

Thus the cultural space is a conceptually manipulative space of possibilities, while social space is the space of action and consensus in which only one possibility is being implemented. If persons only coexist in the physical space without any transactions among themselves, there is obviously only a physical space. If there is a great interval density in their transactions, the social space is sparse, or in other words small. If there is disagreement and lack of consensus, the social space is also small. The social space grows when there is an increase in their collective actions.

The cultural space on the other hand is promoted by disagreement and conflicting opinions, and reduced to a smaller size if there is an agreement. Therefore, we can say that both spaces stand to each other in an indirect dialectical relationship, i.e., one increases at the expense of the other. Both spaces exist within the framework of physical space though they differ from the physical space by their dynamic nature.

Relating group RB and social and cultural spaces, we observe that RB appears more frequently in the social space. A person sharing daily experiences with another person, is able to predict his RB in regard to the chains with which he is familiar. Roughly speaking, there are two major chains, work and home. The group RB tends to be characterized by social structure elements, i.e., part elements, as defined in Chapter III, that enter into RB. These part elements account for the fact that the definition of the personal behavioral RB never completely overlaps with the group definition of behavioral RB. Moreover, the group behavioral RB also shows certain differences given by the different roles observers occupy. Certainly, a maintenance man would give a somewhat different description of RB of a physicist than his colleagues. As a matter of fact, the maintenance man can identify items that are totally absent from the personal RB.

The consensus can then be maintained only if the number of items identified in the RB is reduced; in other words, by means of abstraction particular RB are described in most general terms, and by that the cultural space is reduced. This illustrates what was said above about the contradictory tendencies of both spaces. From the viewpoint of the maintenance man, the scientist has been engaged in RB over a long period of time. From the viewpoint of the scientist or his colleagues there was permanently new IB emerging during his laboratory work; however his colleagues were sharing with him on this point his cultural space in which new items could be identified.

The above example should illustrate the structure of relations between social space RB and cultural space RB. First, there are chains of RB in the social space that are not identified by all persons. A wife, for example, can say only that the husband's RB at a particular time is "work" without specifying more items. In other words, the consensus in definition of RB is achieved, as stated above, by abstraction. If one recalls old theories of social progress such as those of Spencer, Bagehot, Nowicow and others who advanced a thesis about a gradual replacement of physical struggle by a struggle of ideas, it appears that within our framework of discourse there is a similar social system consensus but a cultural multiplicity. We can say that by being socially organized, performing according to the increasingly more rational norms of social space, man can gain more freedom in the cultural space.

Generally speaking, though the social space in fact stands or falls with recurrences and a certain stability of mutual expectations, there is never total consensus among members of the social space in regard to a particular RB. The consensus is only approximate because of the variability of behavioral phenomena and because of differences in their observation. A total consensus can be achieved only in a cultural space if phenomenal elements are completely abstracted. Thus, we have here a paradoxical conclusion, namely that although the cultural space thrives on dissent, merely within its realm can there be achievement of an absolute consensus. On the other hand, within the social space which stands and falls with consensus, the latter can never be absolutely achieved. The consensus in the world of experience is merely approached by raising the level of abstraction.

Probability of Recurrence and Cycle and Patterns of Group RB:

The RB can recur and yet not be perceived by other persons. Though in a small discussion group *à la* Bales, persons have rather adequate definitions of RB, in larger groups respondents do not interact permanently with the pertinent person and consequently do not perceive all his chains of RB. It can be said that only in highly interlocked chains of RB can a person predict what another person is likely to do. The interlocked RB is an RB whose realization is conditioned by the cooperation of another person. If there is not such a strong interrelationship, no such prediction can be made. In most instances there is a great deal of interval density in a particular RB of a person as seen by observers. One could by analogy say that as no single individual ordinarily attains a complete overview of the workings of a community, as pointed out by Dykman, similarly no single individual would ordinarily be able to predict the whole series of RB of a particular person.[22]

If the interdependence between activities of persons is great, as is the case in most work organizations which display a division of labor, then RB cannot only be well predicted by other persons but also can be stipulated by explicit norms. Here the probability of duration of RB or intervals, the probability of being on time, etc., the probability of performing particular chains of RB are all very high, in fact for most work RB is higher than for RB in non-work groups. The most conspicuous example of such a highly probabilistic RB is certainly work on an assembly line. Here the RB has reached such a degree that persons seek to escape either by day-dreaming or by seeking to introduce some variations in the rate of their work.[23]

It appears that industrial sociology findings in regard to monotonous work are quite relevant to this discussion, especially in regard to shifting levels and cycles within which RB can appear. If a man is kept only within one cycle, RB tends to become humanly meaningless. Man craves occasional shifts of the levels of abstraction on which cycles of his RB are carried out, in addition of course to IB. The interval density appears then as a "functional requisite" of a social system. A too tight functional interlocking of particular RB of two persons leads to the deterioration of the social relationship. We are inclined to argue that there is a need for a certain "redundancy," as the term is used in information theory,[24] if the system should operate properly. In our case the redundancy is made up by interval density. The problem which has not been solved, however, even theoretically, is how much interval density is an optimal amount.

Turning now again to the group behavioral RB, let us once

more shortly look at the problem of consensus. It is convenient to differentiate three major types of consensus that could be called central tendency, bi- or more-modal consensus, and irregular or absent consensus.

The central tendency consensus, represented best by the normal curve and its variations, can be expected to be the most common type of consensus of a group in regard to a particular RB. It is also rather unlikely that a mentally healthy and normally socialized person would differ too much in his personal RB from the group RB. Theoretically, however, there is one enticing problem: namely, under what conditions personal RB would not coincide with the group mean RB? For all practical purposes, we do not have any data on such problems that might reveal new perspectives on particular occupational groups as compared with others or as compared with kinship groups or voluntary groups, etc.

A bi- or more-modal distribution- though probably not more than a three-modal distribution- can be expected to occur in a conflict relationship within the group that splits persons into two camps. Also if certain interpretative items are involved in the identification of RB, then there are two group RB referring to the same phenomenon. While items identifying RB are different, the interval and duration usually are the same. Differences in perception of time which are due to social class as reported for example by Leshau, Strauss and Schatzman, to name just a few, would approximate the case.[25] Likewise differences in time perception of persons experiencing anxieties as compared to a non-anxiety group would be relevant.[26]

As irregular group definition of RB or absence of such a definition would indicate in fact that the repetitive behavior is not quite satisfactorily accessible, or that it simply does not attract sufficient attention.

If one looks now at the levels of cycles within which the group RB come into existence, there can be a differentiation of five major levels which can be represented by five types of groups. First, there is the family-work cycle of 24 hours. This is the most basic and frequent set of RB. The work cycle would be represented by work organizations. Though it runs also in a 24-hours cycle, not all days should be included here. In other words, while the family cycle is regular because it is organized around bio-logically derived RB, the work cycle is partially irregular. It should be noted, of course, that the family cycle does not necessarily imply actual families alone, since persons also live alone. Perhaps an even more adequate description of the family cycle is given in terms of spatial propinquity between certain persons or particular facilities, as suggested in another reference by M. Titiev.[27] The voluntary groups cycle comes next. This would be a cycle of weekly or monthly activities such as church, clubs, etc., attendance. The anniversary cycle covers all events happening within the yearly cycle or so. And finally, the life cycle covers events of individual entries and departures from life. From the standpoint of the individual the life cycle is not an RB but IB. As stated earlier, from the viewpoint of society, that can be sometimes developed by persons, the individual vital cycle is a generation RB cycle.

Compared to personal RB, the group RB appears more homo-geneous, being frequently separated from each other distinctly in time as well as in space. It is noteworthy that the temporal cycles and their specialization and concentration in particular social groups tend to be reflected, to some degree in the physical space. Certainly churches or graveyards, etc. are attended within longer cycles than family houses and the like. However, it is the individual who moves not only through different specialized physical spaces but also through different levels of cycles. The heterogeneity is experienced by the individual person himself who in this way can transcend the group pressure toward con-formity. Durkheim adequately argued that an increasing division of labor promotes individualism and a notion of freedom.[28] One could go further by proposing that not only the division of labor but also, if not mostly, the human participation in different time cycles promotes a person's autonomy and ability to transcend his environment.

Group Image RB:

The discussion of RB₁ thus has led one to conclude that it overlaps with IB. In fact, it seems that not too much can be said about the RB₁ that is carried away by streams of consciousness. Off-hand, one would say that even less can be said about the group image RB, i.e., about how members of the group identify a person's RB₁. Here, the old traditional epistemological problem of social science struggling for objectivity of a "covert phenomenon" overshadows the support we have from the difference between conceiving and performing. While a RB₁ is a performance regardless of its relative inaccessibility from other persons, the group image RB is not a performance but only a conceptualization. One should make allowance, of course, for all processes of empathy and their specific forms as suggested theoretically by Max Scheler, George Herbert Mead, and later examined empirically by Renato Tagiuri and others.[29] Since each of us is steeped in his personal flow of time, whose personal nature gains momentum especially in the RB₁, it follows that observers will never be able to participate adequately in the performance flow of RB₁ of another person. More frequently, observers conceive of a person's RB₁ but they do not practice them themselves. In order to induce them to perform RB₁ too, it would be necessary to apply special stimuli that are summarily called aesthetic symbols of fine arts and literature and music.

If the observers tend only to conceive of another person's RB₁, they most likely fall back on cultural definitions of such analogies. Consequently, here again is the paradoxical finding, stressed earlier, namely: that only in cultural definitions can genuine consensus be achieved. In other words, the temporal units items are abstracted and the parts structure is conceptualized. However, since the social space introduces idiosyncratic items, only the cultural abstraction can establish a genuine consensus.

There is one more important point to be underlined in the cognitive process of group image RB. While usually in a stimulus-response relationship a person by analogy assumes that another person responds to the stimulus in a similar manner, in the RB_i the situation is not so easy, simply because there is not a stimulus as such. Especially if the person is engaged in his RB_i in shifting levels of abstraction with their corresponding cycles, observers have hardly any possibility of tracing the person's temporal image track. Again cultural expressive symbols here can be of considerable help. One can assume that much in the same way as a linguistic term plays a considerable influence in the definition of motives, literary and other expressive symbols shifts of temporal cycles facilitate an imaginative reconstruction of a person's RB_i.[30] Probably differences between cultures, difficulties experienced with translation of poetry, etc., are due to some differences in norms on shifting of RB_i cycles.[31] Even though there is a great deal of IB going on, in order for any new IB item to be comprehensible, a considerable amount of RB items must be flushed around. See for example, content analysis of Shakespeare's imagery which disclosed that certain terms and images were frequently recurring in Shakespeare's works.[32]

Following the earlier differentiation between personal past or future RB_i we can also identify group past or future image RB. If one accepts Minkowski's proposition that a man is essentially oriented toward the future,[33] then it would follow that the group image RB is more frequently future-bound. Persons by analogy are more able to differentiate more items in the group future-RB than group past-RB. However, one should make allowances for age. As the life cycle approaches its end, persons tend to practice more past RB_i, and therefore by analogy they should be more adequate in developing group past image RB than the future counterpart. In general, we assume that similarities between the persons and observers who develop the group RB, promote more adequate group image RB.

Conclusion:

In concluding this chapter it is important to underline the variable degree of differentiation between the four categories of

RB discussed here. It goes without saying that the most differentiated, and in that sense most frequent RB is the personal behavioral RB. As stressed earlier, the person is the scene where especially different cycles of RB confront each other. Due to this confrontation a person succeeds in developing transcendence of his immediate environment, which results in the value of freedom. Comparatively the group behavioral RB is limited to fewer cycles, i.e., is more homogeneous. Moreover, the group behavioral RB is more limited to only particular chains of RB. It is the person who moves from one group to the other and who integrates in his memory different personal behavioral RB. By that the person is also stimulated to develop a stronger RB_i. It was pointed out that the personal and even more, the group image RB, compared to behavioral RB are considerably less structured. By overlapping with IB, they are the source of innovation and change.

In this chapter concepts of social and cultural spaces were compared and opposed to each other. However, despite the reference to social and cultural items, RB has not yet been fully discussed as a social relation phenomenon. The group RB were mostly conceived of as a sum of individual values, i.e., summarized consensus. No interaction between persons in regard to RB has yet significantly been considered. This will be the task of the next chapter.

NOTES

1. Barker, *op. cit.*, pp. 1–22.

2. Marvin Harris, *The Nature of Cultural Things* (New York: Random House, 1964) See especially pp. 36–132.

3. Pitirim A. Sorokin and Clarence Berger, *Time-Budgets of Human Behavior* (Cambridge, Mass.: Harvard University Press, 1939), pp. 27–33.

4. This is the so-called Ward study whose data were reproduced by Sebastain de Grazia, *Of Time Work and Leisure* (New York: The Twentieth Century Fund, 1962), p. 444.

5. This is an Opinion Research Corporation study reported by de Grazia, *op. cit.*, pp. 462–463.

6. J. Dumazedier, "Loisirs ouvriers en Europe," *Revue Française de Sociologie* 1963 (4), No. 1, Janvier-Mars, pp. 12–21.

7. J. E. Ross and L. R. Bostian, *The Time Use Patterns and Communication Activities of Wisconsin Farm Families in Wintertime* (Madison: Department of Agricultural Journalism, College of Agriculture, University of Wisconsin) Bulletin 28, March 1958. The Ross and Bostian study also combines the two categories into one mixed category of work and leisure; J. Kazda, Některé otázky mimopracovního času dne," *Ekonomický časopis* (10), No. 3, 1962, pp. 233–255. A good list of references of American rural population studies of time use can be found in L. R. Bostian and J. E. Ross, *Mass Media and the Wisconsin Farm Family* (Madison: University of Wisconsin, 1962). Research Bulletin of the Agricultural Experimental Station No. 234.

8. See Murray Yanowitch, "Soviet Patterns of Time Use and Concepts of Leisure," *Soviet Studies*, July, 1963 (15), No. 1, pp. 17–37. A good survey can also be found in Polish by Alexsander Matejko, ed., *Człowiek i technika współczesna* (Warszawa: Wydawnictwo Związkowe CRZZ, 1964), pp. 63–96.

9. Sebastian de Grazia, "The Uses of Time," in Robert W. Kleemeier, ed., *Aging and Leisure: A Research Perspective into the Meaningful Use of Time* (New York: Oxford University Press, 1961), p. 126.

10. The frequency definition of probability, sometimes also called objectivistic, is "obtained by observation of some repetitions of the event, and from no other source whatsoever." See Leonard J. Savage, *The Foundations of Statistics* (New York: John Wiley, 1954), p. 3. On the same page Savage lists also 'personalistic' and 'necessary' views of probability.

11. See Szandor Szalai, "Rozważanie o czasie," *Studia Socjologiczne* (4) No. 1, 1965, pp. 173–193. See also V. Aubert and H. White, "Sleep: A Sociological Interpretation," *Acta Sociologica* 1959–61 (4 and 5), pp. 1–14, 46–54.

12. John G. Kemeny and J. Laurie Snell, *Finite Markov Chains* (Princeton, New Jersey: D. Van Nostrand, 1960), pp. 43–68.

13. There can be found cultural differences in this connection: Hindus report troubles within a framework of 10–15 years, while Moslems tend to refer to a framework of a week. See Pars Ram and Gardner Murphy, "Recent Investigations of Hindu-Muslim Relations in India," *Human Organization*, 1952 (11) No. 2, pp. 15–16. See also L. B. Brown, "Religious Belief and Judgment of Brief Duration," *Perceptual and Motor Skills*, 1965 (20), pp. 31–34. Characteristic for the time distortion are observations of former unpleasant activities being reported as more pleasant after an elapse of time. See A. C. Kerckhoff, ed., *The Reaction of a Group of Former Air Force Lieutenants to Two Years of Civilian Life* (Technical Report, Air

Force Personnel and Training Research Centre, Lackland Air Force Base, Texas, ASTIA, Document No AD 152–126), p. 232. See also Rudi Supek, *Omladina na Putu Bratstva: Psiho-sociologija Radne Akcije* (Beograd: Mladost, 1963), pp. 201–240.

14. Lylan Lewis, *Blackways of Kent* (Chapel Hill, N.C.: The University of North Carolina Press, 1955), p. 291.

15. See Jiri Kolaja *et al.*, "An Organization seen as a Structure of Decision-making," *Human Relations*, 1963 (16) No. 4, pp. 351–357. About Jaques' seminal concept of discretion and delay in implementation of decisions, see Elliott Jaques, *Measurement of Responsibility: A Study of Work, Payment, and Individual Capacity* (London: Tavistock Publications, 1956), pp. 32–42.

16. Michel M. Borwiecz, *Écrits des condamnés à mort sous l'occupation Allemande* (1939–1945) (Paris: Presses Universitaires de France, 1954). See also W. T. Stace, *Time and Eternity: An Essay in the Philosophy of Religion* (Princeton: Princeton University Press, 1952), pp. 4–6.

17. See, for example, Benedetto Croce's four negative definitions of beauty, i.e., definitions that say what art is not. Benedetto Croce, *Breviř estetiky* (Praha: Orbis, 1927), pp. 61–74. Similarly Gabriel Tarde, *The Laws of Imitation* (New York: Henry Holt, 1903), p. 347.

18. Somewhat similar differentiation was made in regard to terms of 'image' and 'plan'; the latter is closer to implementation, and in that sense similar to our two-layers-present. See George A. Miller *et al.*, *Plans and the Structure of Behavior* (New York: Henry Holt, 1960). Not only mentally affected persons, but also persons who are socially isolated distort significantly their time perception. See S. Goldstone, *et al.*, "Sociometric Status and Apparent Duration," *Journal of Social Psychology*, 1963 (61), pp. 303–310.

19. E. Minkowski, *Le Temp Vécu: Études Phénoménologiques et Psychologiques* (Paris: Collection d'évolution Psychiatrique, 1933), pp. 279–283.

20. Parsons, *Theories of Society*, Vol. II, *op. cit.*, p. 964.

21. Znaniecki, *Cultural Sciences, op. cit.*, pp. 310–327.

22. John W. Dykman, "Of Time and the Plan," *Journal of the American Institute of Planners*, 1962 (28), pp. 141–143. The reference is made to p. 142.

23. See Charles R. Walker ed., *Modern Technology and Civilization: An Introduction to Human Problems in the Machine Age* (New York: McGraw-Hill, 1962), pp. 81–136. Kerr and Keil report results that seemingly contradict our assertion. According to their results the time-drag was estimated by employees to be greater in the variety-type than in the repetitive-type jobs. W. A. Kerr and R. C. Keil, "A Theory and Factory Ex-

periment on the Time-Drag Concept of Boredom," *Journal of Applied Psychology,* 1963 (47), pp. 7–5. However, the finding can be explained as a function of a distracting rather than interesting job. The distracting job does not allow much day dreaming, and therefore it appears as longer than the monotonous job which permits day dreaming. As an evidence see R. H. Knapp and H. B. Green, "The Judgement of Music-filled Intervals and Achievement," *Journal of Social Psychology,* (1961) (54), pp. 263–267. See also R. Kastenbaum, "The Structure and Function of Time Perspective," *Journal of Psychological Researches,* 1964 (8), pp. 97–165.

24. Claude Shanon and Warren Weaver, *The Mathematical Theory of Communication* (Urbana: The University of Illinois Press, 1949), p. 104.

25. L. L. Leshau, "Time Orientation and Social Class," *Journal of Abnormal and Social Psychology,* 1952 (47), pp. 589–592; A. Strauss and L. Schatzman, "Cross-Class Interviewing: An Analysis of Interaction and Communicative Styles," *Human Organization,* 1955 (14), pp. 28–31. See also H. S. Becker and J. Carper, "The Elements of Identification with an Occupation," *American Sociological Review,* 1956 (21), pp. 341–348; Lawrence Frank, "Time Perspectives," *Journal of Social Philosophy,* 1939 (4), pp. 293–312.

26. See, for example, Jonas Langer et al., "The Effect of Danger upon the Experience of Time," *American Journal of Psychology,* 1961 (74), pp. 94–97; Samuel I. Cohen and A. G. Mezey, "The Effect of Anxiety on Time Judgement and Time Experience in Normal Persons," *Journal of Neurology and Neurological Psychiatry,* 1961 (24), pp. 266–268; A. Hoffer and H. Osmond, "The Relationship Between Mood and Time Perception," *Psychiatric Quarterly Supplement,* 1962 (36), pp. 87–92; R. D. Hare, "The Estimation of Short Temporal Intervals Terminated by Shock," *Journal of Clinical Psychology,* 1963 (19), pp. 378–380. In all these studies anxiety produced an impression of longer time.

27. M. Titiev, "The Importance of Space in Primitive Kinship," *American Anthropologist,* 1956 (58), pp. 854–863.

28. Durkheim, *The Division of Labor in Society, op. cit.,* pp. 403–404.

29. Renato Tagiuri, "Relational Analysis: An Extension of Sociometric Method with Emphasis upon Social Perception," in A. Paul Hare *et al.,* eds., *Small Groups: Studies in Social Interaction* (New York: Alfred A. Knopf, 1962), pp. 246–252.

30. See for example C. W. Mills thesis that motives are words, and that without words motives would not be identified. This is of course the James-Lange theory of expression and emotions as well as the George Herbert Mead thesis about the social determination of the self. C. W. Mills, "Situated Actions and Vocabularies of Motive," *American Sociological Review,* No. 6, December 1940 (5), pp. 904–913.

31. For example, Hall reports that in Latin America personal interaction distance is shorter than in the United States. Edward T. Hall, *The Silent Language* (Greenwich, Conn.: Premier Books, 1962), p. 209. See also his chapter "The Voice of Time," pp. 23–41.

32. C. F. E. Spurgeon, *Shakespeare's Imagery and What it Tells Us* (New York: Macmillan, 1936), p. 309 and ff.

33. Minkowski, *op. cit.*, p. 279.

V A FEDERATION OF RB

As surveyed in Chapter III, the concept of social system appears to have been not only generally accepted, but also its relationship to other terms such as "structure" has been defined. By placing a new term, i.e., "federation" in the title of this chapter, one runs the danger of introducing unnecessarily a neologism. This chapter purports, however, to justify the use of the new term. A considerable degree of looseness between phenomena, i.e., a considerable degree of interval density calls for a term that should not convey the idea of close interlocking of parts, as conveyed by the notion of system.

This chapter also seeks to develop RB as a social phenomenon, starting with the interaction of two persons and ending with interactions of large aggregates or groups. In the third and last section of the chapter, the issue of federation of social RB as compared to that of social system will be taken up.

RB of Two Interacting Persons:

The analysis in Chapter IV has identified behavioral and image RB. Moreover, behavioral RB could occur in five major cycles. Altogether, we have six different categories of RB, if both behavioral and image RB are combined. If two persons interact, there could be theoretically 36 combinations of each person's category with the other person's category. Though the image RB can occur, in combinations in which one person emits behavioral RB only, while the other person practices image RB, it is unlikely that both could interact and yet practice different behavioral cycles. The reason is that cycles, as shown in Chapter IV, specialize usually in terms of locales, personnel, etc. This certainly reduces the number of possible combinations.

Our major interest in this section is attached to the problem of IB in an interaction between two persons. What instances can be differentiated?

When two persons interact, each having a somewhat different probability of rank orders of RB chains, they can influence each other by introducing IB. A person who gets an IB from another person can either let it run through and let it disappear again, or he can accept the IB and turn it into RB. We are interested in the latter case. Under what conditions is an IB emitted by one person accepted by another person?

Theoretically, four possible cases can be differentiated. Let us assume that the IB emitter is high in IB while the receiver is low in IB. Vice versa, one can assume that the emitter is low in IB while the receiver is high in IB. The question is whether a person who is more productive in IB is also generally more receptive to another person's IB than a person who is low in producing IB. Before resolving this question, one should of course attach the usual *ceteris paribus* condition. Then one can propose that a low producer of IB is not likely to induce IB in another person, especially if the other person himself is a high producer.[1] Thus the innovation flows mostly from a high emitter of IB. As far as the receiver is concerned, it appears that the receiver is more likely to obtain IB from the emitter if he himself is also a high emitter, than if he himself is a low emitter. Since a high emitter of IB keeps his own RB chain set changing, it is easier to accept another person's IB than if there is little change. In other words it is proposed that from the four possible pairs, the similar pairs are at extremes; either very high in influence, if both of them are high emitters or very low, if both are low emitters. Mixed pairs appear to be between these two extreme cases.

The high IB persons are of course persons who have many RB with a low probability of recurrence. Accordingly, one can raise another very important question: if a person's activity is very frequently repeated but with a low probability, what influence can he have on another person with similar or different values on the criteria of frequency and probability? To facilitate the discussion of possible instances, let us employ the following table:

Table 1

CROSS-CLASSIFICATION OF TWO PERSONS ON PROBABILITY
OF RB AND FREQUENCY OF RB

Person A　　　　　　　　　　　　　　　　　　Person B

Frequency of RB

	Low (High IB)	High (Low IB)	Low (High IB)	High (Low IB)
Low Probability of RB	1A	2A	1B	2B
High	3A	4A	3B	4B

In the above table it is assumed that frequencies of RB for both persons A and B occur within the same cycle. Then the problem is which combination is more influential among the cells with high IB, i.e., cells 1 or 3. Note that this time it is not possible to propose that the extreme cells, i.e., cells 1 and 4, are also extreme in influence. In cell 4 there should be a few IB while in cell 1 there should be many IB; since cell 1 indicates a rather unpredictable type, Person B is also unlikely to be influenced by A's many IB. In that sense I would like to qualify the former proposition that great emitters of IB are likely to influence other persons; a condition of a certain degree of predictability of A's behavior must be present in order that his influence should be effective. This is met by cell 3 rather than by cell 1.

The prior proposition placing a premium on order rather than frequency is very important.[2] It means that while frequency is primarily rooted in the biological sphere of human existence, the order, the being "on time," i.e., the cultural norm gains importance in social context. In reference to the discussion of biologically rooted and culturally derived chains of RB in Chapter IV, it appears that one can expand as follows: while biological processes such as blood circulation and their recurrences are extremely frequent, and "on time," frequencies of biologically derived RB are still frequent but less "on time." But cultural RB display both frequent and infrequent recurrences as well as great or low predictabilities. Theoretically, if there is also an increase in IB, there will also be a greater functional requirement for a greater predictability in RB. Moreover, if there is another person involved, there will be an even greater increase in predictability if the interaction system has to work. One could postulate that this functional requisite increases with an increasing number of persons though the relationship is unlikely to be linear. An increase in "being on time" that results from interdependencies, can be increased only up to a certain point after which the marginal law of diminishing returns sets in.[3]

Returning to table 1, let us explore possibilities of combining cells of both persons A and B. It should be remembered that we are assuming that the interaction between A and B is an ongoing process, and that consequently only IB can bring innovation. Without the assumption, two persons who have just started interaction for the first time could borrow RB from each other and accept them within their personal rank order RB set as an IB.

Examining first cognate cells in both A and B cells, pairs will be ordered according to an increasing degree of influence, as follows:

Table 2

PAIRS OF A AND B CELLS ACCORDING TO
THE DEGREE OF INFLUENCE

The least influence	2a — 2b
	4a — 4b
The greatest influence	1a — 1b
	3a — 3b

The rank order indicates that theoretically we assume that both a low number of IB, i.e., a high number of RB, and a low probability, i.e., a relative absence of order, promote a low degree of influence, and vice versa. While the low number of IB criterion is almost self-explanatory, the probability criterion earlier discussed, calls for one more additional comment. Certainly the 1a-1b pair shows both persons producing a high number of IB. However, the relative lack of order promotes a situation in which IB are traded, but rarely retained. They just pass through B in order to disappear. In 3a-3b pair the IB tend to be retained, and in that sense the influence of A upon B can be considered greater.

Turning to influences of A upon B by means of noncognate cell pairs, all combinations can be eliminated right away in which 2a and 4a are emitters. Only those in which 1a and 3a emit influence are of interest. Following the same criterion of influence, the highest influence occurs when 1a and 3a emit to 3b and 1b respectively. In other words there is a tendency to increase influence if the non-cognate cell is approached within the low RB frequency column.

We have so far considered interaction between two persons only in regard to behavioral chains of RB. Moreover, each person was conceived of as performing his own set of RB and IB, and only occasionally accepting an IB from the other person. Suppose now that we also introduce image RB, and that both persons are engaged in interlocked RB. In such a situation an IB must be classified as such by both persons.

In the interlocked RB the personal RB can then be realized only by means of image RB, though, there can also be an image interlocked RB when both persons share their RB_i. These are certainly rare moments but one should acknowledge that these are interactions of an extremely powerful interlocked RB, exemplified for example by lovers and such like. In most instances while the interlocked behavioral RB is going on, the image RB serves to free the person from a steady attendance of the interlocked RB. One can observe that rules for behavioral RB usually serve to introduce a greater interval density within the RB. As Theodore Geiger points out, it is usually easier to develop agreement on procedural rules than on the contents of bargaining.[4] As stated earlier in the previous chapter, the consensus in the social space provides for a possible heterogeneity in cultural space; Crozier has recently proposed that rules provide for a greater autonomy of subordinates.[5]

RB and Aggregates and Organizations:

The major portion of the RB theory will be dealt with in this section. Keeping in mind the time-space framework, we generally conceive of society as chains of individual RB, interspersed with IB that run across individual RB à la Tarde as waves of innovation. The chains of individual RB can run either parallel to each other, or they can be organized into interlocking RB. In developing additional necessary concepts, MacIver's concepts will be found helpful.[6]

MacIver has differentiated three categories of actions that he called distributive, conjunctural and collective. In the distributive actions persons act on their own without attention to each other. One could probably conceive of all bodily maintenance activities RB as distributive actions. If a larger unit such as a family would be taken as one part, then all the activities within the family household, usually termed private activities, could be classified as distributive. Chains of RB that run distributively (parallel to each other) make up probably the largest block of waking time consumed by persons.

In the conjunctural action persons are not organized but conceive of consequences of certain activities of their own as well as of other persons. One could say that according to Max Weber, these activities are genuine social activities because awareness of other persons' actions is present. It appears that the conjunctural action is similar to the image RB in our system. There is clearly an element of transcendence of the immediate behavioral situation. Note however, that in the conjunctural case persons still act individually, and that they only reflect on the cumulative effect of their individual actions.

Once persons get organized and introduce a certain division of roles in order to reach a particular objective, they have attained collective actions, according to MacIver. This would correspond to our interlocking RB as far as RB are concerned.

A further reflection upon MacIver's categories reveals an interesting affinity with our three types of space: distributive actions happen within the physical space, collective actions are to be located in the social space, and finally the conjunctural category would find an approximate coordination within the cultural space of possibilities, although MacIver did not mean by his concept only a conceptual manipulation of potentialities but also manifested behavioral implementation of the chosen alternatives.

A further examination of MacIver's categories also discloses that there no attention is given to time as such. Categories predominantly refer to "space," or at best to future-bound actions. A predominant orientation is synchronic, and therefore one can ask what would happen if an asynchronic perspective were induced?

First, it is necessary to point out that all three of MacIver's categories also can be applied to one person action only. While a person acts in a group, he emits phases of activities that are in fact distributive, intermittently conjunctural or collective. Suppose a bricklayer works on a construction. In some phases of his work time flow, he works for some moments by himself, in other phases he estimates whether other bricklayers keep the same pace as he does, in other phases he coordinates his movements with a supplier of bricks.

If this is true about individual persons and small groups, then by extrapolation one can assume that the same holds true about the relationship between aggregates of persons or social organizations. Thus one can propose that aggregates pass through distributive phases exemplified by breakfasting, through conjunctural phases exemplified by driving to the place of work, and finally through collective phases exemplified according to whether they are predominantly engaged in one of the three activities. So, productive organizations could be conceived of as distributive, marketing organizations as conjunctural, and different control governmental organizations as more collective function organizations.

Moreover, it appears that one can differentiate two structures here: first, there are aggregates of persons who are engaged in producing their chains of RB. Asynchronically, they pass through three stages for example during the morning in which their parallel RB gradually become more interlocking RB. If the interlocking RB is the most genuine expression of Society, capitalized *à la* Durkheim, then one could say that society arouses itself gradually from a distributive phase through conjunctural toward a collective phase, i.e., the genuine social phase. Within the family group cycle of 24 hours, referred to earlier, society then gradually deploys itself in order to later return to its more distributive phase, ending in the suspension of society, i.e., in the majority's distributive sleep. One could in fact compare society to a rhythm of tide and ebb.[7]

While the above ebb-tide scheme of phases is extended along the temporal dimension, the organization structure based upon specialization according to certain functions is extended spatially. The structure, composed of MacIver's action-types, appears when society is fully deployed, i.e., during the collective work phase. If one would visualize the 24-hours cycle of the whole society, he would perceive the following figure.

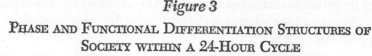

Figure 3

PHASE AND FUNCTIONAL DIFFERENTIATION STRUCTURES OF
SOCIETY WITHIN A 24-HOUR CYCLE

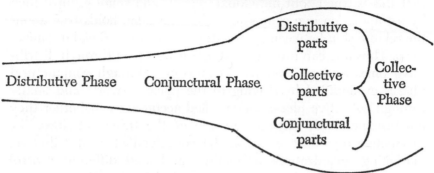

The above enlargement of the Collective Phase brings to one's mind the former discussion on the status of time and space in the conclusion of Chapter I and Chapter III. It appears as if society would spatialize itself, extend itself along the parts axis at the peak of the day cycle, while the temporal units phases prevail at the beginning and at the end of the day cycle. It is clear that from the viewpoint of society the interval density is great in distributive and conjunctural phases-time units- while it is smallest in the collective phase. Within the collective phase it is further smallest within the collective part as compared to the distributive and conjunctural parts.

While it is true that in the evening the differentiated and organized structure of the collective work period recedes to that of a relatively distributive behavior, there is one major exception to this trend. Mass media provide for unique, if not collective then at least conjunctural actions of attention to their programs. In a national program of significance to many persons, a considerable number, if not the majority of adult persons, can be urged to participate in it. Of course, the participation is passive and distributive. In a large majority of different organized leisure activities most persons "consume" without producing any tangible or symbolic items that would establish their relationship with other aggregates or organizations as happens in work activities.

Let us review for a moment the use of MacIver's categories. It has been proposed that all three of the categories can be found in one person's action as well as in a 24-hours day of an aggregate of persons. One should acknowledge that the inspiration of this observation is derived from Parsons' theory of action whose four well-known functional problems can be presumably identified on personal as well as societal levels. The difference between the four categories of Parsons and our three categories is that Parsons treats his categories in a more or less synchronic perspective while we have an asynchronic approach. The three phases follow each other. Note however, that while in one person's action there will be eventually many phases, i.e., many RB of the three categories, in the 24-hours cycle of a large aggregate we have differentiated only two RB of the same phase, in the morning and in the evening. This means that with the increase in the number of persons, the phases appear to have become longer but also consequently less frequent.

The above observation is of utmost importance. Below there will be made an attempt to demonstrate that with the increasing scale, the frequencies of certain RB occur more rarely. Why is it so? The answer must be sought in structural changes due to division of labor. We have already noticed above that within the 24-hours cycle there were two structures developed along temporal or spatial dimensions. The second was in fact due to the division of labor, i.e., to the spatial parts structure. While society exists in recurrences along the time dimension, by means of the division of labor, society has been moved from asynchronicity toward synchronicity. In a maximum division of labor structure everything that previously had to be done consecutively, could be done at the same time, at least theoretically.

Let us turn our attention to longer cycles such as week cycles of voluntary groups or anniversary cycles. We can observe here that MacIver's three categories have not been completely eliminated if one conceives of RB on the levels of these cycles. The meeting itself can be considered as the collective phase while all other activities that occurred in the period between weekly or anniversary meetings could be conceived of as distributive from the viewpoint of the group that meets. However, the group that meets is not "the total society" or at least a majority of all adult persons. In most instances in voluntary groups or in anniversaries such as birthdays these are partial or small groups with the exception of some events of national significance to be discussed below.

It appears that week-end days do not achieve such a high division of labor as work days, and consequently within the weekly or anniversary cycles there is no such synchronization of collective RB as there is in the 24-hours cycle. There are of course specialized agencies of government that take care of long cycles RB. Possibly, there is only one major large cycle collective RB, i.e. elections. One should note that in the election process masses do not passively attend as in mass media reception, but they actively participate. Note that this type of organized mass participation happens rather infrequently, not even in each annual cycle. And this leads one to a major consideration on the relationship between the number of persons and the frequency of RB.

The Number of Persons and Frequency of RB:

In this section special attention will be paid again to Durkheim whose assertion about a positive relationship between division of labor and frequency of sacred RB will be examined. Using MacIver's concept of collectively organized actions, it is proposed as follows:
Proposition No 1:
The more frequently a greater number of persons perform a particular RB, the less collectively organized this RB will be.
And from this we can advance as follows:
Proposition No 2:
The greater the number of persons actively participating in one organized collective RB, the less frequently this RB will occur.

These two propositions constitute the core of the RB system on the societal level. Essentially, they challenge the Durkheimian proposition by maintaining just the opposite of what Durkheim did. Due to internalization and socialization there is no need for an organized national agency to bring about a synchronic RB such as Sunday morning church attendance. Students of political sociology such as Kornhauser have stressed that a democratic society cannot be well developed if RB are frequently organized on the societal level.[8] Within this context the example provided by totalitarian societies, in which more RB involving more persons are organized by one agency, could be interpreted as a case of insufficient institutionalization and internalization. One could argue that such frequent collective RB become insignificant for their members.[9] Though thousands of small discussion groups meet to consider the program offered by the Party, the meetings acquire a ritualistic character. On that point they could be classified as instances of passive participation similar to passive RB of mass media consumers. The reference to significance that is certainly small in such meetings, leads to proposition No. 3:

If the significance of collectively organized RB is greater, a greater number of persons actively participate in them.

In light of proposition No 2 above, however, one must conclude in proposition No 4:

The more significant a collectively organized RB is, the less frequently it occurs.

This proposition then challenges Durkheim's assertion. However, to do justice to Durkheim, let us remember that he referred not only to frequencies but also to a "being on time" criterion.[10]

Proposition No 5, however, is somewhat in agreement with the latter point:

A collectively organized and more significant RB is also more on time in its recurrence than a less significant collectively organized RB.

Note that proposition No. 5 converges with whatever was said earlier about the time precision in RB as being characteristic of cultural RB more than of biological RB.

Reviewing the five propositions, we can conclude that collective RB tend to recur less frequently. There is definitely more interval density between their recurrences. Since society has a large scope as compared to a small group of persons, one can observe here a tendency of convergency between social space and length of intervals between units of RB. Society, in its collectively organized RB tends then to recur less frequently than RB in small groups. There is a parallel with the personal RB set. In the personal RB set those chains which recur in long cycles, appear also to be more remembered than frequent RB. Could one say that the memory of RB indicates its significance? But significance in regard to what?

Frequency of RB and Their Relative Significance:

The subtitle raises one of the most difficult problems in sociological theory. The answer attempted here should be accepted therefore as tentative.

If one would fall back upon the funtional theory he could propose that that item is more significant whose removal will disturb or stop a greater number of parts or RB temporal units. Note that in fact we answer the question of functional significance on both dimensions developed in our discussion so far, i.e., the spatial as well as the temporal dimensions.

The problem is however that social phenomena treated by us so far have been placed within different spaces, or as some authors would call it, different levels of reality. Obviously, the significance on one level of reality is not exactly the same as another. The significance of frequencies in physical space does not correspond to frequencies in social space, and even less so in cultural space. The break between significances in these three spaces is probably best conceptualized by theories of emergent evolution represented in philosophy, for example, by Smuts, in sociology by Spencer and in psychology by Maslow.[11] Generally, it is assumed that the new "higher level" has emerged when the lower level was completely developed (principle of plenitude according to medieval philosophical cosmology),[12] or when needs of the level were satisfied, and the phenomenon was ready to make new advances, or be further advanced.

The discussion of this RB theory has hardly equipped us to deal with problems connected with the theory of emergent evolution. For the sake of further development of the RB theory, let us accept that frequencies occur in all of the three spaces but that their significance is not the same, though it is similar. Somewhat reminiscent of the negative heuristic explanation in aesthetic theory, it appears that we at present can do nothing but offer an explanation more in negative than positive terms.

When further examined, there are two points on which a more positive description perhaps can be provided: first, one can fall back upon the entropy theory and argue in terms of organization. Secondly, one can arrange the three spaces hierarchically in the sense that the physical space will be "at the bottom," and other spaces higher according to higher levels of abstraction.

In previous chapters the notions of interval density and degree of porosity have been used. Generally speaking, one can propose that since phenomena are related to each other with different intensities, one can differentiate between structures and systems. As defined earlier, the system indicates a higher degree of organization, i.e., a lower entropy. The lower the entropy, the more significant is the central position and, less significant, provided that a *ceteris paribus* condition is attached, is the frequency of RB. Conversely, the more phenomena approach by their relationships a loose structure, the more significant frequencies become.

The above generalization, reached independently of the previous discussion of the scale and frequencies, converge surprisingly with proposition five. The more significant something is, the more persons participate, but the less frequently it occurs, provided that it is a collective action.

The level of abstraction does not appear to contradict the above finding either, to say the least. Frequencies are cognate with the physical space more than with the social, and even less cultural space. It appears both ontogenetically and socially, that the more a person is developed, the more he tends to abstract, to transcend attention to the immediate present. It follows, then, that while the social space is less affected by frequencies than the physical space, it is on the other hand more affected than the cultural space. Though values of the cultural space had also been developed as a result of frequencies of experience, the relationship between them and frequencies has become less clear. This is probably why many thinkers following the Platonic example have tended to declare values timeless or time transcendent. From our viewpoint this is inadmissible. Values are also realized in recurrent frequencies, and though the significance of the frequency is not entirely clear at present, at least not as clear as it is in the physical and social space, we are not inclined to discard it. At present, let us submit only that the frequencies within the cultural space would have a somewhat different frame of reference than frequencies in physical and social spaces.

Productive and Consummatory RB:

Let us now return to the prior analysis of the distributive categories and collective organizations within a 24-hours cycle. Interestingly, if one also keeps in mind the yearly-cycle, one can conceive of all voluntary weekly and monthly collective actions as distributive units in regard to the major anniversary collective action identified as a political action, i.e., election. Though in general all RB can be classified either as distributive or collective (provided that at least two persons are involved in an interlocking RB), it is suggested that one differentiate the two major categories of RB in society. Between them, one can place a semi-collective conjunctural RB manifested in passive consumption of a mass media product. Visualizing it, the following figure emerges:

Figure 4

COLLECTIVE 24-HOURS CYCLE AND ANNIVERSARY CYCLES RB AND SEMI-COLLECTIVE RB

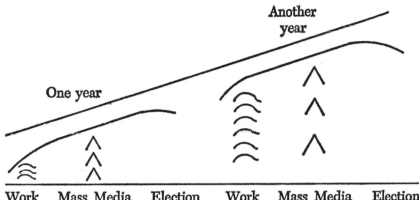

Work   Mass Media   Election   Work   Mass Media   Election

In order to visualize variables let us report that the two curve shapes convey the idea that election takes place at the end of each year. Furthermore, the semi-collective character of social phenomena is represented by triangle forms (mass media reception), the collective character by curves (work). Mass media attendance is more individual than work organizations that bring together many persons. Note that the election is represented by a long curve that covers longer periods.

Generally, we have here a structure of gradual encapsulation of smaller units by larger units. Semi-collective triangles of mass media reception and small curves representing work activities make up the long curve of election. The figure seeks to comprehend differential time rates of daily, weekly, or yearly processes. Sociological theories have not been too much concerned with different speeds and dimensions within which particular processes in society occur.

The above figure could also be conceived of as a structure of consuming and productive RB. While the family distributive RB would be classified as consuming, the collective RB would be clearly productive. Mass media for the majority of RB would be consuming, while the anniversary political RB should be conceived of as productive like probably most, but not all voluntary groups RB. Then the whole flow of RB appears as two major chains of, productive and consuming RB.

Following the analysis in terms of productive and consuming RB, we are led to postulate that there should also be productive and consuming phases within the voluntary group weekly-monthly cycles. In other works, within the three major cycles to which reference has been made in this analysis, RB should be differentiated according to the two production-consumption axis. Not only that, the production consumption pair figuratively corresponds to the systola diastola of the blood flow, i.e., to the basic metabolic biological process. But physiological processes influence a person's psychological time perception, as reported by Thor. Past and future events appear less distant at mid-day than at early A.M. or late P.M.[13] The difference between biological systems and RB structures is that the social RB are differentiated along many more axes than just along the production-consumption axis.

Age Aggregates RB and Organizational RB:

In the discussion of distributive RB, no attention has been directed to persons who perform those RB. Since time perception depends to some degree on age and socio-educational characteristics, a consideration of these aggregates is in order here. We can conceive of these age and other aggregates as structures which cut across, respectively, distributive, conjunctural and organizational productive and consummatory phases or structures of RB.

Considering the criterion of age, one is struck by its distributive character. A similar distributive character can be found among other characteristics of social structure such as sex, education, health, income, occupation. Only to some degree are these distributive characteristics organized collectively.

The fact that society is composed of individual persons who

in a distributive manner show different characteristics is one of
the problems not faced within the theory of social systems.
Following our differentiation of phases, one can propose that the
collective phase tends to replace "ascriptive" characteristics of the
distributive phase by "achievement" criteria. Since many of the
distributive ascriptive criteria are derived from biological properties of persons, one can also argue that in the collective
phase the biological foundation of society has been overcome,
and that persons in a truly Durkheimian way have spiritualized
themselves, i.e., have achieved their "selves" in social relations
only.[14]

Concerning age groups, we know that they show differences
in time perspective. For example, Wallach and Green found that
older persons selected metaphors that described time in dynamic
terms while younger persons chose metaphors expressing tran-
quility.[15] (see TRB in figure 5.) For young persons TRB appears
long while for old persons short. Another investigation by Feifel
corroborated the fact that time appears to pass quicker for older
persons than for young ones.[16] And yet older persons tend to
perform most activities in a slower way than younger persons
who show an opposite tendency. Consequently, there is here an
interesting distortion of physical time. Probably persons in the
middle of the age gradient show the least deviations in terms
of psychological time as compared to physical time, and in terms
of performance of activities. Figure 5 shows the relationship
between the young and old age aggregates.

Note that in the above figure one line refers to future RB_i
and past RB_i. Through we do not have any research evidence,
one may assume that younger persons tend to produce more
future RB_i than past RB_i and vice versa for old persons. Consequently, it appears that at least on three criteria notions of
temporal properties or of time itself appear to be significantly
different for both extreme age categories.

What significance do the age categories have? One can observe
that there are no social organizations that would express the
time perception differences. There are two reasons for this: first,

Figure 5

YOUNG AND OLD AGE CATEGORIES AND PSYCHOLOGICAL TIME
AND PHYSICAL TIME

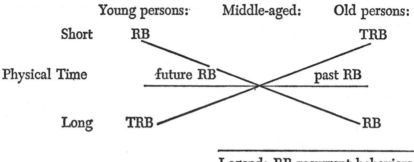

Legend: RB recurrent behaviors
TRB Psychological
Time of RB

the differences are not so great that they would interfere with the functioning of organizations. Moreover, the physical time is binding for both young and old. Secondly, there is a continuum between both extreme age categories. Perhaps if there were only young persons and old persons, differences in time perception would be organizationally expressed. But there is the large "middle-aged" category that usually wields considerable power in most organizations. Therefore, in all collective image RB of the past, collective anniversaries such as Memorial Day,[17] there is only one organized event for all age categories together. It is worth noticing that tribal societies were more differentiated along the age categories lines than we are today, as shown for example by Monica Wilson.[18] Urban rationalization has tended to break down most ascriptive criteria. Though this has been a general trend, so well described from different viewpoints by Weber as well by Durkheim and others, it is quite possible that future trends might somewhat reverse these tendencies.

It has been stated earlier that society primarily has only "all-societal collective" memorial events; and yet young persons are more likely to think in terms of future RB_i than older persons. Most of our memorial national events are post-bound RB. As the rate of social change increases and as the planning of a collective future gains more ground, there might also appear collective future-bound RB instead of predominant past-oriented RB. Socialistic and communist movements have in fact provided examples such as the collective future-bound RB of the First May. However, like other memorial RB, it appears that the First May also is gradually becoming a collective memory of the past instead of the future. Among the few future-bound RB it appears that the future element is probably more preserved in the quickly disappearing peasant festivals welcoming spring. In modern societies there are collective inauguration festivals that serve as collective IB; the next year, if they are remembered, they become collective RB. The only strongly future-bound semi-collective event is New Years Day, mixed however with reviews of the past year. According to our former discussion of the relationship between the number of persons and the frequency of collectively organized RB, one could point out that the rarity of the future-bound collective event is a function of its collective nature. This would be plausible, provided that we would also have only one or two past oriented RB. Moreover, one should note that the New Year RB like church attendance on Sunday, is not really collectively organized from one center. The problem of one-center collectively organized events and the problem of system will be discussed in the following section.

Social System and Federation of RB:

So far two major dimensions have been frequently referred to: the temporal and the spatial. The degree of relationship between temporal units as well as between spatial parts was described by notions of porosity, interval density, and MacIver's three categories of distributive, conjunctural and collective actions. It has also been pointed out that the theory of social system as usually discussed by sociologists has been mostly concerned with the synchronic relationship between parts; moreover, little attention, if any, has been paid to the differential degree of the relationship.

Let us assume that we have two structures: one in which the spatial structure parts react to each other almost instantaneously; the other, asynchronic, in which parts react to each other successively. It means that the more society is differentiated into different subsystems, the less likely will there be a simultaneous interaction between all parts. The interaction is then more developed along the temporal dimension. It is interesting to note that if simultaneity and succession are considered in terms of cultural and social spaces, there result two opposite tendencies. In the cultural space simultaneity can be achieved for all possible items only if all persons available would subscribe and practice different items and activities in order to exhaust at least in an approximate manner all potentialities. Such a cultural simultaneity would be possible only if there were almost an absolute tolerance and if almost all persons or small groups were engaged in distributive actions. In other words it would be possible if there were few collective actions that require standardization.

If one recalls that cultural space has been defined as the potential number of items that can be successively actualized, it appears that simultaneity is incompatible with the cultural space. The latter can thrive only in successive actualization of selected items.

Applying conversely asynchronic succession to the social space, again there results a case of incompatibility. It means that actions would be going on only in particular items while other items were immobilized until their turn would come. Social process would be thus extremely slowed down, and social organization would be very inefficient.

Obviously, the above two references are nothing but theoretical instances that indicate limiting positions. However, these theoretical extreme cases indicate a need for "tolerance" within the cultural space. In order that different items may co-exist, a considerable degree of co-existence conditions must be present, i.e., considerable isolation, or as Robin Williams has appropriately explained it: insulation of items or their particular groupings must be developed.[19]

While the cultural system tends to isolate units from each other in order to actualize as many items as possible, the social system tends in an opposite direction, to relate parts in simultaneous connections that, however, are standardized and interlocked. Since both tendencies can not be achieved at once, a compromise between both must be brought about. Figure No. 6 is offered as an attempt to visualize the midpoint between both cultural diversity but lack of connections, and social uniformity but a higher degree of interconnections.

Figure 6

AXIS OF CULTURAL AND SOCIAL SPACES

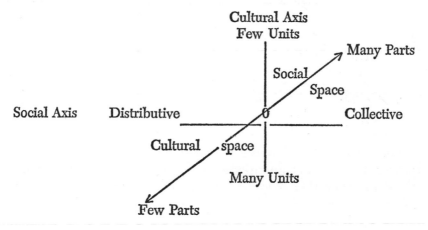

In the above figure the double-headed arrow indicates the opposite tendencies discussed above. How are these conflicting tendencies resolved? There are the two basic structures that help to develop enough room for both tendencies, namely the spatial parts based upon the division of labor, and the temporal units containing a greater number of chains of RB. In both structures the viable position is achieved by means of greater interval density.

Figure 7

INTERVAL DENSITY ON PERSONAL CHAINS RB AXIS, ON
FREQUENCY OF RB AXIS, AND ON THE
DIVISION OF LABOR AXIS

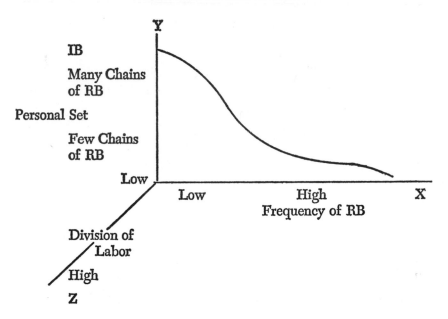

Note first that within the personal set of RB (axis Y) the S curve reaches its maximum when many chains of RB change into IB. Remember that a great number of chains would overload memory and a person would consequently classify many RB as new, i.e., IB. Otherwise the figure expresses the usual statement about the impact of the division of labor that results in more repetitive and more particularized activities. There are more particularized activities. There are more different chains of RB (axis Z) performed by more persons, but fewer persons perform many different chains (axis Y). This indicates the earlier visualization of the collective organized phase as an enlargement or as a spilling over of society into simultaneous spatial structure. However, if there are fewer chains of RB per person, there will be a greater tendency to compensate with RB_i, and in general with more porosity of actions, or even more interval density. This is somewhat surprising because one would assume that a high frequency of RB does not leave too much room for internal density. Note however, that a high frequency is related to a higher division of roles, i.e., a greater interdependence between chains of RB performed by different persons. More persons, however, tend to develop a greater variety of cultural items and individual idiosyncrasies that can be encapsulated only by introducing greater spatial and temporal insulation. Our argument should of course be interpreted within a somewhat larger framework of division of labor than that represented by an assembly line. However, even at the assembly line, if there is a greater number of items related in interdependence, there is also a greater likelihood that there will be an interference with the total flow because of the greater probability of a breakdown of at least one item.

Thus the argument here is that greater frequency of particular RB chains is achieved at the price not only of introducing a greater porosity within the RB phenomenon itself, and also by introducing greater interval density between particular chains of RB. This holds true if the performances should not be interfered with too frequently because of a lack of temporal or spatial coordination.

Interestingly, the three axes of Figure 7 could also be compared to cultural, social and physical spaces discussed earlier. The number of RB or IB would be the cultural, the number of frequencies the physical space, and the division of labor the social space. Certainly such an analogy involves considerable risk, since from another viewpoint, the frequency and the division of labor could be reversed as well in regard to physical and social spaces. But what is more rewarding is that within Figure 7 all three spaces tend to be related to each other functionally, which, ultimately means also quantitatively.

The above conclusion leads us then to the proposition that the term "federation of functions" better corresponds to the phenomenal reality called society.[20] Within the federation of functions there are organizations that can more appropriately be described by the concept of system. Most work organizations would fall here because of their performance criteria, definite interlocking RB, an imposed limited cultural space dominated by the collective organization of the social space. If the former discussion of distributive and collective phases, and production and consumption structures is recalled, it appears that their mutual relations can also be visualized by the following figure.

Figure 8

DISTRIBUTIVE (CONSUMPTION) AND COLLECTIVE (PRODUCTION)
PHASES OF A 24-HOURS CYCLE

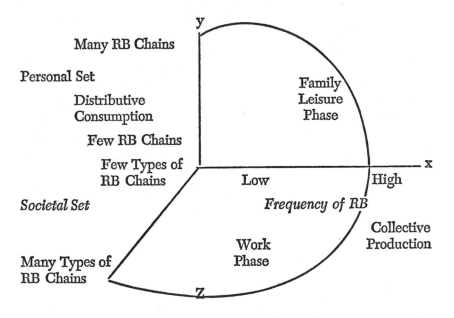

Figure 8 again shows a similar relationship to that of Figure 7, this time however between personal distributive RB, and societal types of RB, and Collective Production RB. In order to differentiate between chains of a person and chains of a society, the term type has been introduced. Obviously within one type there are similar chains of many persons. Though differentiated from the viewpoint of the person, within the societal frame of reference particular personal chains are encapsulated with the type category. Following the encapsulation principle, one could further extend figure 8 to larger temporal units such as those of voluntary groups or anniversary events cycles. Then collective RB of a daily cycle should be conceived of as distributive RB in regard to the collective yearly cycle (e.g., election). Note that these different RB cycles are carried by the same present, and that they are separated from each other by different interval density. Consequently, the whole federation of these cycles is based upon suspension and actualization.

In the conclusion of Chapter IV we have already noticed that the multiplicity of temporal cycles accounts for the development of the value of freedom. Here one could go further by maintaining that the multiplicity of cycles is related to levels of abstractions, to the ability of shifting from concrete levels to more abstract levels; in other words, to conceive of society as a hierarchy of levels of parts and cycles of units. This means ultimately to conceive of society as an invisible whole, as a unit. The additional point to be made however, is that this all-embracing unity is an intermittent phenomenon. That not only individual but also social life is a rhythm of uniformity and individuality. In the individual image RB we have sought the source of IB. Moreover, it has been proposed here that the two phases can be identified on several levels that are hierarchically organized, encapsulating each other. Society in this respect then appears as a federated hierarchy of encapsulated spatial parts and temporal units.

NOTES

1. Elihu Katz and Paul F. Lazarsfeld, *Personal Influence: The Part Played by People in the Flow of Mass Communications* (Glencoe, Ill.: The Free Press, 1955), pp. 321–334.

2. The daily repetitive life imposes a certain order, a certain economy that reduces waste of nature, as has been pointed out by a stimulating analysis of daily recurrencies by Henri Lefebevre, *Critique de la Vie Quotidienne,* (Paris: L'Arche Éditeur, Vol. I, 1958, Vol. II, 1961). The reference is made to Vol. II, pp. 356–357.

3. George Caspar Homans, *Social Behavior: Its Elementary Forms* (New York: Harcourt, Brace & World, 1961), pp. 265–282.

4. Theodore Geiger, *Debat med Uppsala om Moral Og Ret* (Lund: C.W.K. Gleerup, 1946), pp. 52–61 (in Swedish).

5. Michel Crozier, *The Bureaucratic Phenomenon* (Chicago: The University of Chicago Press, 1964).

6. Robert M. MacIver, *Social Causation* (Boston: Ginn, 1942) pp. 292–302.

7. The tide-ebb cycle has been extensively studied not only by human ecologists but also by regional geographers, and transportation engineers. To illustrate these studies, only a few are listed here: Kate K. Liepman, *The Journey to Work: Its Significance for Industrial and Community Life* (London: Kegan Paul, Trench, Trubner, 1944); J. E. Spencer, "The Szechwan Village Fair," *Economic Geography,* 1940 (16), pp. 48–58; J. Ellis Voss, *Summer Resorts: An Ecological Analysis of a Satellite Community* (Philadelphia: The University of Pennsylvania Ph.D. Dissertation, 1941); A. H. Hawley, *Human Ecology: A Theory of Community Structure* (New York: The Ronald Press Co., 1950), pp. 288–316; Duan F. Marble, "Transport Inputs at Urban Residential Sites," *Regional Science Association Papers and Proceedings,* 1959 (5), pp. 253–266.

8. William Kornhauser, *The Politics of Mass Society* (Glencoe, Ill.: The Free Press, 1959).

9. Alex Inkeles, *Public Opinion in Soviet Russia* (Cambridge: Harvard University Press, 1958), p. 83.

10. Emile Durkheim, *The Elementary Form of the Religious Life* (Glencoe, Ill.: The Free Press, n.d.), p. 367. Durkheim speaks of a greater regularity. I interpret it as a greater "precision."

11. A. H. Maslow, *Motivation and Personality* (New York: Harper, 1954).

12. David Bidney, *Theoretical Anthropology* (New York: Columbia University Press, 1953), p. 41.

13. D. H. Thor, "Time Perspective and Time of Day," *Psychological Record,* 1962 (12), pp. 417–422; D. H. Thor, "Diurnal Variability in Time Estimation," *Perceptual and Motor Skills,* 1962 (15), pp. 451–454.

14. Durkheim, *op. cit.,* pp. 415–447.

15. M. A. Wallach and L. R. Green, "On Age and the Subjective Speed of Time," *Journal of Gerontology,* 1961 (16), pp. 71–74. It should be reported also that Survillo found that time was found not to move faster with

advancing age. See Walter W. Survillo, "Age and the Perception of Short Intervals of Time," *Journal of Gerontology*, 1964 (19), pp. 322–324. On the other hand, Alexis Carrel as early as 1931 stressed that during old age time appears to pass quicker. See A. Carrel, "Physiological Time," *Science*, 1931 (71), pp. 618–621.

16. H. Feifel, "Judgement of Time in Younger and Older Persons," *Journal of Gerontology*, 1957 (12), pp. 71–74.

17. Lloyd W. Warner, *American Life: Dream and Reality* (Chicago: University of Chicago Press, 1953), pp. 1–26.

18. Monica Wilson, *Good Company: A Study of Nyakyusa Age-Villagers* (Boston: Beacon Press, 1963).

19. Robin M. Williams, Jr., *American Society: A Sociological Interpretation* (New York: A. A. Knopf, 1952), p. 532.

20. The term "federation of functions" was probably first used in the literature by A. Bláha. Recently, the concept of federation appeared in Fred E. Katz, "Explaining Informal Work Groups in Complex Organizations: the Case for Autonomy in Structure," *Administrative Science Quarterly*, 1965 (10), pp. 204–223.